The Rational Consumer

The Rational Consumer: Theory and Evidence

Robert E. Hall

The MIT Press
Cambridge, Massachusetts
London, England

This book was set in Times Roman by Asco Trade Typesetting Ltd., Hong Kong and printed and bound in the United States of America.

Library of Congress Cataloging-in-Publication Data

Hall, Robert Ernest, 1943–
  The rational consumer: theory and evidence/Robert E. Hall.
    p. cm.
  Papers written 1967–1989.
  ISBN 0-262-08197-0 (hc)
  1. Consumption (Economics)—Econometric models. 2. Taxation of articles of consumption—United States—Econometric models.
I. Title.
HB801.H284   1990
339.4'7—dc20

90-13336
CIP

Contents

Introduction

My work on consumption started in 1966 when I was a graduate student at MIT. Optimal growth was a hot topic at the time, and I became interested in the interpretation of the optimal growth model as a model of life-cycle consumption behavior rather than as the behavior of a social planner. I worked within what have remained the two standard intertemporal models of consumer behavior—the overlapping generations model and the infinite lifetime model. Most of the implications I drew from these models dealt with public finance.

The first chapter in this volume is a seminar version of longer material from my Ph.D. thesis, reprinted here without any modification. (I am grateful to Joe Stiglitz for providing me with a copy that turned up when he moved to Stanford; the paper had long since disappeared from my files.) This version gives a reasonably detailed exposition of the proposition that Robert Barro made famous in the mid-1970s: a policy of government borrowing today with taxes in the future is no different from a policy of taxing today, because rational consumers will fully offset the deficit with increased saving. I was told that this neutrality proposition was well known from the work of Edmund Phelps, but today the credit is given to David Ricardo.

While I was an undergraduate at Berkeley and during my first summer in graduate school, I worked with Dale Jorgenson on his theory of investment. My contribution was to improve the treatment of taxes in the model. In 1966, Jorgenson and I presented a study of effects of changing the investment tax credit to the U.S. Treasury. The audience included James Tobin, who pointed out that our model assumed that the world believed that all changes in the tax credit were permanent, even when they were explicitly announced to be temporary. I went back to MIT and worked out what became the second chapter in this volume, "The Dynamic Effects of Fiscal Policy in an Economy with Foresight" (published in the *Review of Economic Studies* in 1971). The foresight that matters is the foresight of consumers, so this paper is really an exercise for the life-cycle model where consumers know in advance about important jumps in their economic environment. In 1973, Robert Lucas, in his famous critique of econometric policy evaluation (published in 1976), criticized my work with Jorgenson as failing to meet the test of rational expectations. The 1971 paper, in effect, made the same criticism. Perfect foresight models can be seen as approximations to rational expectations models. My Hoover colleague Ken Judd has made great progress in giving a full rational expectations treatment with uncertainty to this type of problem.

One of the first pieces of research I did after arriving at Berkeley to teach in 1967 appears here as chapter 3, "Consumption Taxes versus Income Taxes: Implications for Economic Growth." The essential issue here is intertemporal substitution. The paper compares steady states in an economy where consumers have long but finite lifetimes. Taxing the return to savings is a significant handicap in an economy with a fair amount of intertemporal substitution.

The work in part I all predates the rational expectations revolution. During my tenure on the MIT faculty (1970–77) I worked mainly on labor market issues. But when the revolution occurred—I would date that event around 1974—I was drawn back into general equilibrium macro in general and consumption economics in particular. One morning in January 1976 I was pondering the consumption function in a vest-pocket macromodel I had developed for studying public finance and energy issues. It suddenly occurred to me that the natural specification of the consumption function was to make consumption depend on the actual present discounted value of future income. Up to that time, practical consumption functions had followed Albert Ando and Franco Modigliani in building a model of expected future income based on current and lagged variables. The MPS model had an elaborate and carefully reasoned consumption function of this type. But rational expectations teaches as that the best model of expectations is the whole general equilibrium model. Except for departures from certainty equivalence, the right answer is to put the actual income forecast of the model into the consumption function. Under Lucas's influence, many econometricians have adopted this procedure for treating expectations wherever they occur.

At the time I resumed work on consumption in 1976, I was familiar with empirical tests for efficient securities markets and the connection of that research to rational expectations. I noticed that exactly the same principle applied to consumption. There is an isomorphism with the stock market. Future income has the same role as future dividends, and consumption is the analogue of the stock price. In the stock market, the current stock price aggregates all information about the future; no other variable apart from the price should help predict the future price. So, current consumption should aggregate all information about future consumption. To put it differently, consumption should be a random walk. I quickly ran some regressions that showed that there was very little predictive power for future consumption not contained in current consumption.

The first draft of what is reprinted here as chapter 4, "Stochastic Implications of the Life Cycle–Permanent Income Hypothesis: Theory and Evidence," was less than a smash hit. Stan Fischer, who was spending the year in Jerusalem, wrote back to ask what psychoactive substance was affecting me as I wrote and to suggest that the paper badly needed a serious theory section. With this guidance, I was able to get it published in the *JPE* in 1978. Now that thousands of papers have been written using the Euler equation approach, it is hard to remember the reaction of established consumption function veterans. There was a great deal of confusion between a structural consumption function and the first-order condition of a consumption theory. My equation was disparaged as lacking in explanatory power in comparison to those with a rich set of contemporaneous explanatory variables. But in the following decade, structural consumption functions came to enjoy a peaceful coexistence with Euler equations.

Rick Mishkin, who wrote a Ph.D. thesis on consumption at MIT at the time that I was working on the random walk, joined forces with me to study consumption in panel data. Chapter 5, "The Sensitivity of Consumption to Transitory Income: Estimates from Panel Data on Households," is the result of our collaboration. We showed the failure of the random-walk implication in data on individual households and went on to build a structural model with a transitory component of consumption. The component is partly random and partly associated with transitory income.

Very soon after the publication of the random-walk paper, it became apparent that its general tone in favor of the absence of predictive power of lagged variables other than consumption itself was mistaken. Marjorie Flavin, who had been my research assistant in writing the paper, went on to do important research of her own, showing that there was important predictive power in certain lags of real disposable income that I had failed to test. Her interpretation was that some households do not obey the dictates of the life-cycle model. But another possibility was that predictable changes in consumption occur because of intertemporal substitution. My 1978 paper assumed constant expected real interest rates. Consumers who respond to higher interest rates by deferring consumption could violate the random-walk property and yet be complying fully with the requirements of life-cyle rationality.

Chapter 6, "Intertemporal Substitution in Consumption," is the result of nearly a decade of sporadic work on this topic. I became aware of work by finance economists that seemed to provide the right framework for thinking about the joint behavior of consumption and interest rates. But in finance theory, the focus is on risk aversion, whereas I was interested in intertemporal substitution. The problem is that the natural model with time-separable preferences locks risk aversion and intertemporal substitution together. Consumers who care a lot about risk are also very reluctant to depart from an even allocation of consumption from one year to the next. My intuition was that the equation I was interested in, which made the expected growth of consumption depend on the expected real return to saving, revealed information about intertemporal substitution and not about risk aversion. I fiddled with various theoretical arguments along this line, but the problem was solved by a number of theorists just in time to get into the published version of the paper.

Chapter 7 is a survey of work on consumption in the general area of the random-walk paper, commissioned by Robert Barro for his volume on modern business cycle theory.

Almost all research on consumption concludes that there is an element of the time-series behavior of consumption not explained by the life-cycle model. Chapter 8 is an attempt to quantify that component and to measure its significance as a driving force for the business cycle. The basic idea is that the same forces that make the public consume more goods should make them consume more leisure as well. When consumption falls at the same time that employment falls, it is unlikely to be the response of households to events in another sector. Instead, it is probably a spontaneous shift in consumption. Positive comovements of consumption and work have been relatively common in U.S. experience.

I THE FARSIGHTED CONSUMER UNDER CERTAINTY

1 The Allocation of Wealth among the Generations of a Family That Lasts Forever: A Theory of Inheritance

Recent models of economic growth have been based on a variety of assumptions about consumption behavior. First, a large literature has grown out of the assumption that consumers make decisions by arbitrary rules, particularly the rule of consuming a fixed fraction of total income or that of consuming all wages and saving all profits. Second, in the past 2 or 3 years there has been a resurgence of interest in models of optimal accumulation in which consumption behavior is regulated by an authority that can see far beyond the lifetime of any individual and that maximizes a social welfare function defined over the consumption of present and future generations. Finally, an important series of papers by Samuelson (1958), Diamond (1965), and Cass and Yaari (1965) have investigated competitive models in which individuals determine their consumption for two or more periods by maximizing a utility function subject to a wealth constraint. The results of these investigations are somewhat disturbing—in particular, the competitive equilibrium interest rate may be permanently less than the rate of growth because of oversaving. This implies that the equilibrium is inefficient by a well-known theorem of Phelps and Koopmans (1965). Further, as Diamond has shown, some seemingly neutral fiscal activities of the government may have an important effect on the equilibrium—there may indeed be a "burden" of the public debt.

These models neglect an important aspect of the intertemporal decisions of the consumer—namely, that a person usually cares not only about his own consumption but also about the well-being of his children. A father has a considerable amount of control over his sons' wealth because he can vary the size of the bequest that he makes to them. In this essay I derive some of the implications of hypothesis about the way in which a family makes decisions about inheritance. The hypothesis is that a father and his sons decide jointly how to allocate their wealth between the father's and the sons' consumption by maximizing a utility function in which each one's consumption appears as an argument. Interestingly, while the spirit of this hypothesis is similar to that of the competitive utility maximizing models of Samuelson-Diamond-Cass-Yaari, the properties of the resulting model are very much like those of the centrally directed social-welfare-maximizing models of optimal growth. In fact, I will demonstrate that this competitive model has the catenary turnpike property common to almost all models of optimal growth.

This essay treats a highly stylized economy in which there is one kind of output, which may be either consumed or used as capital in production.

Each person lives two periods but consumes and earns wages only in the second period. At the beginning of the second period each person marries and has $1 + n$ sons and $1 + n$ daughters. A family consists of husband and wife, their children, and all their future descendents. There is a perfect market for loans between any two periods. Production is carried out by profit-maximizing entrepreneurs who borrow from the public to finance all their investments. Production is assumed to take place with constant returns to scale, and output is sold in a competitive market, so entrepreneurs earn no profit. Finally, all families are assumed to be identical.

1.1   Family Demand Functions with a Finite Horizon

The assumptions of this essay about the family allocation process can be stated in two main hypotheses. First, we have the following.

HYPOTHESIS ON THE ALLOCATION OF WEALTH BETWEEN FATHER AND SON: However much wealth a father and his sons devote to their consumption, they divide it among themselves so as to maximize a joint utility function,

$$U(c_f, c_s),$$

where c_f is the father's (and mother's) consumption and c_s is the consumption of each of their sons and daughters. We further assume that U is quasi-concave.

Then, as a consequence of this maximization process, for any given amount of wealth that they spend in total, there is a unique demand function giving the parents' share, where the parents are now identified as generation t:

$$c_t = d(x_t, r_t); \tag{1}$$

x_t is the present value of the consumption of parents and offspring, and r_t is the interest rate on loans between period t and period $t + 1$.

It is sensible to assume that the parent's consumption is not an inferior good:

$$\frac{\partial d}{\partial x_t} \geq 0. \tag{2}$$

Now if each pair of generations makes its decisions by this process and if the decisions are consistent in that each son's planned consumption is the same as his actual consumption as a father, then the consumption of all future generations can be predicted exactly, given today's parents' consumption. This follows by induction after establishing the uniqueness of the sons' consumption given the parents' consumption, since each son subsequently becomes a father. For this purpose, consider the following diagram:

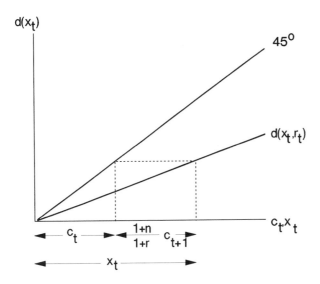

Figure 1.1

To determine the c_{t+1} corresponding to a particular c_t, draw a vertical line up from c_t to the 45° line and extend it horizontally to its intersection with the $d(x_t, r_t)$ curve (the intersection is unique by the assumption that the curve does not turn down). The horizontal distance at the intersection is the total expenditure x_t corresponding to c_t; the consumption per son is given by

$$c_{t+1} = \frac{1 + r_t}{1 + n}(x_t - c_t).\tag{3}$$

Thus the parents can predict the consumption of every generation corresponding to a particular value of their own consumption. Analytically, this can be seen by substituting

$$x_t = c_t + \frac{1+n}{1+r_t} c_{t+1} \tag{4}$$

in equation 1 to get an implicit difference equation,

$$c_t = d\left(c_t + \frac{1+n}{1+r_t} c_{t+1}, r_t\right), \tag{5}$$

which can always be stated explicitly in the form

$$c_{t+1} = g(c_t, r_t). \tag{6}$$

Today's parents can use this relation to predict the consumption of all future generations.

It remains to introduce an additional hypothesis to specify in what way today's parents and offspring care about future generations of the family or, in other words, how they choose the part of the total family wealth that they will appropriate for themselves, x_t. This leads to the following hypotheses.

HYPOTHESIS OF FUTURE GENERATIONS: Today's parents and offspring spend the largest amount of wealth, x_t, that is consistent with the long-run family budget constraint that terminal wealth not be negative.

Then the decision-making process of the family may be visualized in the following way: today's parents and offspring examine the various family consumption trajectories that correspond to alternative values of x_t and pick the value of x_t whose consumption trajectory will exhaust family wealth at time T. The easiest way to state the exhaustion of wealth is in terms of family assets (nonhuman wealth); if A_t denotes family assets per person measured at the beginning of period t, then

$$A_{t+1} = \frac{1+r_t}{1+n} A_t + w_t - c_t, \tag{7}$$

where w_t is noninterest income (wages) per person in period t. Then the budget constraint is

$$A_{T+1} = 0. \tag{8}$$

Because of the continuity of the functions involved, there is always a value of the parents' consumption c_t corresponding to a trajectory that exactly meets this budget constraint.

The discussion so far has considered only the behavior and motivation of one pair of generations of a family and has carefully avoided the notion that any individual made plans that are binding on future generations. It is interesting at this point to investigate the consequences of this kind of behavior for the family as a whole. In particular, we inquire whether or not this behavior is reasonable in the sense that it resembles the behavior that might be prescribed if the family in fact had a planner.

The discussion will draw upon the results of Hall (1967), which proposes a hypothesis that is equivalent to the present one in the special case where the intergenerational utility function has the special additive form

$$U(c_t, c_{t+1}) = u(c_t) + (1 + n)v(c_{t+1}). \tag{9}$$

This form is assumed in the following discussion.

The first important property of family consumption under the inheritance hypothesis is *efficiency*. A consumption trajectory is efficient if there is no generation whose consumption could be increased without violating the family budget constraint. Clearly with a finite horizon any trajectory that meets the budget constraint exactly is efficient; the real significance of this property is apparent only when the family is assumed to last forever. However, family consumption behavior based on arbitrary rules (such as a constant savings ratio) may fail to meet even this simple criterion.

The second important property is what Samuelson (1950) calls *reversibility*: for any consumption trajectory there is a total family wealth and an interest rate trajectory that yields the consumption trajectory as the family demand. In other words, there are no parts of the consumption space that are permanently in the dark in the sense that they would never be the demand of a family in a competitive economy. If a surrogate family utility function exists, this property is equivalent to quasi-concavity of the function. In the present model this property always holds if the horizon is finite. The conditions for family equilibrium are

$$s(c_t, c_{t+1}) \equiv \frac{v'(c_{t+1})}{u'(c_t)} = \frac{1 + r_t}{1 + n} \tag{10}$$

and

$$W = \sum_{t=1}^{T} \prod_{\tau=1}^{t-1} \left(\frac{1 + n}{1 + r_\tau}\right) c_t. \tag{11}$$

Thus the reversibility conditions are satisfied with

$$r_t = (1 + n)s(c_t, c_{t+1}) - 1, \tag{12}$$

and the value of W given in equation 11.

A third property, equivalent to the second if a surrogate family utility function exists, is *diminishing marginal rate of substitution*. This is important because it indicates a tendency for the family consumption plan to involve approximately equal consumption for all generations rather than concentrating on only a few generations. Hall (1967) showed that diminishing marginal rate of substitution will hold in this model if the rate of change of the rate of impatience with respect to the consumption level is small in absolute value. The rate of impatience, $\rho(c)$, is defined by

$$\rho(c) = (1 + n)s(c, c); \tag{13}$$

it is the interest rate at which the level of consumption c will remain constant. Diminishing marginal rate of substitution is guaranteed over any horizon T if

$$\frac{|\rho^o(c)|}{1 + \rho(c)} < \varepsilon, \tag{14}$$

for a positive constant ε, independent of T.

A fourth property of possible interest is the existence of a surrogate family utility function $U^*(c_1, \ldots, c_T)$ with the property that all family consumption decisions could be portrayed *as if* they were made by maximizing this function subject to the family budget constraint. We find from Hall (1967) that in general there is no such surrogate family utility, and hence no meaning can be given to the notion of family preferences among alternative consumption trajectories. This is neither destructive nor, in retrospect, a surprising conclusion. After all, the only connection that today's generations have with the future in this model is a concern for the financial integrity of the family; it would be surprising indeed if this were equivalent to having preferences between any pair of consumption trajectories even when the only difference between the trajectories was in the consumption of a generation far in the future.

There is one significant expectation to this conclusion. If the rate of impatience is constant over all consumption levels, then there is, in fact, a surrogate utility with the familiar form

$$U^*(c_1,\ldots,c_T) = \sum_{t=1}^{T} \left(\frac{1+n}{1+\rho}\right)^t u(c_t).$$

(15)

Then the process of allocating wealth between succeeding generations is exactly the same as would be implied by the Euler equation for maximizing (15); the budget constraint is exactly the transversality condition for this maximization. In this case the inheritance hypothesis amounts to assuming that the family has adopted as its behavioral rule, not the notion of maximizing a utility function, but an operationally identical rule that turns out to be the Euler equation and its transversality condition. This, I think, makes the notion of a family utility function of the special form (15) more acceptable to those who reject the ideal of a family consciously maximizing a utility function on the grounds that there is no central authority within a family who makes and enforces consumption plans.

1.2   Consumption Demand for a Family That Lasts Forever

Economic intuition suggests that the behavior of a family that expects to last a thousand years should be only infinitesimally different from one that expects to last forever. The hypotheses on family behavior proposed in this section are not sufficiently strong to guarantee this irrelevance of the distant future, nor, in fact, are they strong enough to ensure that the criteria of reasonable family demand behavior are met when the family lasts forever. Paradoxically, demand functions that are efficient and reversible for any horizon T, no matter how far distant, may be inefficient or irreversible when the horizon is infinitely distant. Not surprisingly, this is closely related to the problem of impatience. A similar paradox has been observed in models of optimal economic growth (for example, Samuelson 1967), where it has been resolved by showing that impatience is a logical necessity if a true utility function is to exist (Diamond 1965). Thus we may immediately conclude that the inheritance hypothesis implies a surrogate family utility function if and only if $\rho(c) > n$ and $\rho'(c) = 0$ for all c.

The difficulty with respect to the properties of efficiency and reversibility is the following: If there is a c such that $\rho(c) < n$, then either

1. If reversibility holds, the consumption trajectory $c_t = c$ for all t is in-efficient, because the implied interest rate is less than the rate of growth, and a debt incurred by any generation vanishes in the limit,[1] or

2. Reversibility fails. This will happen if $\rho'(c) < 0$; see section 1.3 in this regard.

Thus the inheritance hypothesis must be strengthened in the following way:

HYPOTHESIS ON IMPATIENCE: Either both efficiency and reversibility hold for the consumption demand of a family that lasts forever, *or* (equivalently) the family is always impatient: $\rho(c) > n$. Efficiency is the more important of the first two properties, since it alone implies that the competitive equilibrium involves an interest rate whose limit is at least as large as the rate of growth.

Now we are prepared to discuss the full family wealth allocation problem over infinite time. Stated formally, the problem is to find a first generation consumption c_1 so that for given initial family assets A_1, $\lim_{t \to \infty} A_t \geq 0$, where future consumption and assets are predicted by the pair of difference equations

$$c_{t+1} = g(c_t, r_t) \tag{16}$$

$$A_{t+1} = \frac{1 + r_t}{1 + n} A_t + w_t - c_t. \tag{17}$$

As several authors have remarked, this problem may not have a sensible solution. For example, if

$$g(c_t, r_t) = \frac{1 + r_t}{1 + n} c_t \tag{18}$$

(this comes from a log-linear intergenerational utility), if r_t has the constant value $\tilde{r} > n$, and if $w_t = 0$ for all t, future consumption is

$$c_t = \left(\frac{1 + \tilde{r}}{1 + n}\right)^{t-1} c_1. \tag{19}$$

Family assets at time t are

$$A_t = \left(\frac{1 + \bar{r}}{1 + n}\right)^{t-1} (A_1 - t c_1). \tag{20}$$

For any positive c_1, $\lim_{t \to \infty} A_t = -\infty$. The fact that some interest-rate trajectories make it impossible for the family to allocate its wealth in a reasonable fashion should not cause us to reject this model of family behavior. Rather, it shows how the inheritance hypothesis restricts the form of the competitive equilibrium. For example, if families have a fixed rate of impatience, the competitive equilibrium capital stock will approach a steady state over time such that the net marginal product of capital will exactly equal the rate of impatience. This is discussed at greater length in section 1.3.

1.3   General Equilibrium in the Inheritance Model

Suppose that a neoclassical technology prevails, in which output per person, y, is given by a smooth convex function of capital per person:

$$y = f(k). \tag{21}$$

Capital deteriorates geometrically at a rate δ, so investment for replacement is δk, and investment to maintain the capital-labor ratio is nk. Thus net investment per person is

$$\Delta k_t = f(k_t) - c_{t+1} - (\delta + n)k_t, \quad \text{or} \tag{22}$$

$$k_{t+1} = (1 - \delta - n)k_t + f(k_t) - c_{t+1}. \tag{23}$$

The interest rate is equal to the net marginal product of capital:

$$r_t = f'(k_t) - \delta. \tag{24}$$

Consumption behavior is given by

$$c_{t+1} = g(c_t, r_t). \tag{25}$$

Finally, we have the fundamental budget constraint $A_{T+1} = k_T = 0$. The analysis of this system will be carried out in terms of consumption and the interest rate, although it could also be done in terms of any of several pairs of variables.

The (r, c) phase plane can be divided into two areas according to whether r is increasing or decreasing. The interest rate is unchanged from one period to the next only if k is unchanged, or

$$f(k) = (\delta + n)k + c. \tag{26}$$

In order to characterize this line in terms of r, we differentiate with respect to r:

$$f'(k)\frac{dk}{dr} = (\delta + n)\frac{dk}{dr} + \frac{dc}{dr}\bigg|_{\Delta r=0}. \tag{27}$$

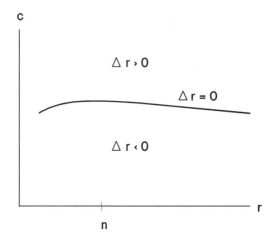

Figure 1.2

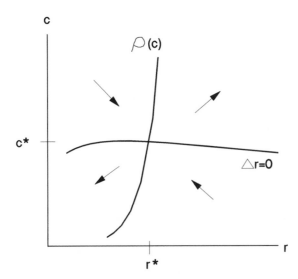

Figure 1.3

Now since $r = f'(k) - \delta$, $(dk/dr) = 1/f''(k)$, and

$$\left.\frac{dc}{dr}\right|_{\Delta r=0} = \frac{f'(k) - \delta - n}{f''(k)}$$

$$= \frac{r - n}{f''(k)} \tag{28}$$

Thus the line slopes upward if $r < n$, reaches its maximum at $r = n$ (the golden rule), and declines if $r > n$; above the line capital is decreasing and r is increasing; the opposite occurs below the line (see figure 1.2):

A similar division of the phase plane is possible for the consumption equation: consumption is increasing whenever $r > \rho(c)$ and is decreasing whenever $r < \rho(c)$. Thus the phase diagram has the shown in figure 1.3.

Since the absolute value of $\rho'(c)$ is restricted to small values, it is reasonable to assume that the two stationary loci meet at a unique stationary point (r^*, c^*). If so, $\rho(c)$ cuts $\Delta r = 0$ from below, the stationary point is a saddle point, and from the catenary properties of a saddle point, the following result is established.

COMPETITIVE TURNPIKE THEOREM. *As the end of the world becomes more distant (as the horizon T becomes large), the competitive equilibrium interest rate–consumption trajectory spends almost all of this time arbitrarily close to the point (r^*, c^*), where the rate of time preference is equal to the stationary interest rate.*

Figure 1.4 illustrates trajectories for various T's, starting with the same initial capital stock. Plotted against time, these have the appearance shown in figure 1.5. The case of an economy that lasts forever is a simple extension of the previous case. The only infinitely long (r, c) trajectories are those running along the top of the saddle, as seen in figure 1.6. From any initial capital stock, the economy eventually approaches indefinitely close to the steady-state point (r^*, c^*).

It remains to show that these trajectories are truly competitive equilibria. That is, we must show that given the interest rate and wage trajectories derived from the phase-plane analysis, family demand would in fact be the consumption trajectory shown. Since these trajectories satisfy the difference equation (25), the conditions on the marginal rate of substitution between consecutive generations are clearly met. Futhermore, if the horizon is finite, terminal family assets are zero, and no generation can increase its consump-

c

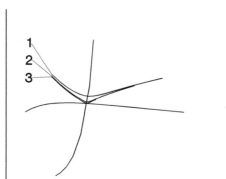

Figure 1.4

c

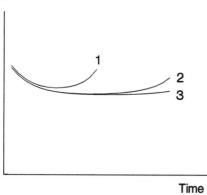

Time

Figure 1.5

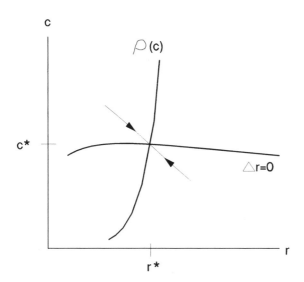

Figure 1.6

tion without decreasing the consumption of another generation. Thus the budget constraint is also met; we conclude that this trajectory is in fact the unique family demand. On the supply side, the assumption that the production function is convex guarantees that the supply of consumption goods is uniquely this trajectory.

With an infinite horizon, the limiting value of family assets is not zero, as it would be if the family could exhaust its wealth, but rather is the value of the steady-state capital stock k^*. However, if all debts must eventually be paid back (that is, if the present value of one unit of income, $\pi_{\tau=1}^{\tau}[(1 + n)/(1 + r_{\tau})]$, goes to zero in the limit), no generation can increase its consumption by even the smallest amount without causing eventual family bankruptcy. Thus, even though family assets eventually always have a large positive value close to k^*, the budget constraint is met, and the trajectory is the true family demand. The requirement that debts must be paid back is crucial. For example, if there is a surrogate family utility function with zero rate of impatience, the present value function does not go to zero and there can be no competitive equilibrium. Given the interest-rate trajectory from the phase-plane analysis, the family will not choose the consumption trajectory shown there, but rather will choose one with higher consumption for one or more generations and for which the limiting value of family assets is not k^* but zero. This is one of a variety of difficulties that arise in an economy in which the interest rate goes to n sufficiently quickly for the present value function not to have limit zero. Most of the hard problems of optimal growth theory are related to this problem; similarly, the interesting aspects of the study of the efficiency of an economy that lasts forever arise only in this case.

One property of the family's allocation problem deserves further attention; it is stated in the following theorem.

THEOREM ON THE IRRELEVANCE OF THE DISTANT FUTURE. *Along competitive equilibrium interest rate and wage trajectories the consumption of the present generation of a family becomes increasingly insensitive to their desired level of assets for generations t, as t increases, provided $\rho(c) > n$. Their sensitivity decreases with increasing impatience and increases with an increasing rate of change of impatience with respect to consumption.*

Proof. The sensitivity of the present generation to future asset levels is measured as the reciprocal of the derivative of A_t with respect to c_1. The system of difference equations governing the allocation of family wealth is

$$c_{t+1} = g(c_t, r_t)$$

$$A_{t+1} = \frac{1 + r_t}{1 + n} A_t + w_t - c_t. \tag{29}$$

Differentiating with respect to c_1, we get

$$\frac{dc_{t+1}}{dc_1} = \frac{\partial g(c_t, r_t)}{\partial c_t} \frac{dc_t}{dc_1} \tag{30}$$

$$\frac{dA_{t+1}}{dc_1} = \frac{1 + r_t}{1 + n} \frac{dA_t}{dc_1} - \frac{dc_t}{dc_1}, \tag{31}$$

with initial conditions $dc_1/dc_1 = 1$ and $dA_1/dc_1 = 0$. Now the function $g(c_t, r_t)$ is defined implicitly by

$$\frac{v'(c_{t+1})}{u'(c_t)} = \frac{1 + r_t}{1 + n}. \tag{32}$$

so

$$\frac{v''(c_{t+1})}{u'(c_t)} \frac{\partial g}{\partial c_t} - \frac{v'(c_{t+1})u''(c_t)}{[u'(c_t)]^2}, \tag{33}$$

or

$$\frac{\partial g}{\partial c_t} = \frac{u''(c_t)v'(c_{t+1})}{v''(c_{t+1})u'(c_t)}. \tag{34}$$

Now c_t approaches the limit c^*, and from Hall (1967),

$$\rho'(c^*) = [1 + (c^*)]\left[\frac{v''(c^*)}{v'(c^*)} - \frac{u''(c^*)}{u'(c^*)}\right]. \tag{35}$$

Thus if $\rho'(c^*) < 0$, there is a T such that $t > T$ implies

$$\frac{u''(c_t)}{u'(c_t)} < \frac{v''(c_{t+1})}{v'(c_{t+1})}, \quad \text{or}$$

$$\frac{\partial g}{dc_t} > 1. \tag{36}$$

Similarly, if $\rho'(c^*) > 0$, eventually $\partial g/\partial c_t < 1$.

In the asset equation, eventually $(1 + r_t)/(1 + n) > 1$, since r_t approaches the limit $\rho(c^*)$, which is greater than n. Because of its simple recursive form, the properties of the system (30) and (31) may be seen by inspection. Since $\partial g/\partial c_t$ is always positive and $(1 + r_t)/(1 + n)$ is eventually strictly greater than one, dA_t/dc_1 becomes indefinitely negative with increasing t. If $\rho'(c^*) < 0$, the contribution of the term $-dc_t/dc_1$ also becomes indefinitely large, whereas in the opposite case, its contribution is eventually zero. But in either case, dc_1/dA_t has the limiting value zero, and the theorem is established.

The property stated in this theorem is also observed in all optimal growth problems with catenary motions; it is sometimes referred to as instability, but this is extremely misleading, since its behavioral implication is one of stability, not instability.

The assumption that the family faces interest-rate and wage trajectories that will turn out to be the equilibrium trajectories is crucial in this theorem. Along other trajectories, there may be a solution to the allocation problem. This will almost always be true if $\rho'(c) < 0$, since any stationary point of equations (29) is an unstable node, with roots

$$\lambda_1 = \frac{1 + r}{1 + n} \qquad \lambda_2 = \frac{\partial g}{\partial c},$$

both of which exceed 1. Usually no trajectory can reach such a stationary point of an asymptotically autonomous system. Along an equilibrium trajectory, however, the interest rate changes over time exactly fast enough to allow the (A_t, c_t) trajectory to reach the unstable node. This means that a *tâtonnement* procedure would probably not be able to find the equilibrium, since it would require families to solve the allocation problem with interest rate trajectories that are not equilibria. In fact, computational experiments have indicated that the family must take account of the effect of its allocation of wealth (and the identical allocation of all other families) on the interest rate in order to obtain a *tâtonnement* procedure that is likely to work. It is possible to show that there is an interest-rate adjustment of a simple form that can be applied by each family and that guarantees convergence to the competitive equilibrium—this adjustment converts the family's allocation problem into one with strictly catenary properties.

1.4   Some Implications of the Inheritance Hypothesis

The most important difference between this and other models of competitive equilibrium with individually directed saving is that each person is required to see some distance into the future because he is sensitive to future economic developments. This has a number of important implications. First, since the family has a rate of preference for the parents' consumption at least equal to the rate of growth, the possibility of an inefficient competitive equilibrium is ruled out.

Second, in this model the equilibrium is independent of the size of the government's debt, so there is no burden of the debt. In Diamond's model, the equilibrium is sensitive to the size of the debt because the market capitalizes all the interest payments that a bond yields, but the individual takes account of only the tax payments to finance the interest that are levied during his lifetime. This asymmetric effect makes him spend more and save less, driving up the interest rate. Under the inheritance hypothesis there is no asymmetry because the individual does not distinguish between his own wealth and the wealth of the future generations of his family. The equilibrium is independent of any transfer of wealth between generations and in particular is independent of the transfer implied by taxing and paying interest.

Third, this model resolves a perplexing question about the competitive equilibrium price for an asset that cannot be produced, such as land.

Nothing in the equilibrium condition for the market for such an asset prevents an upward speculative movement in its price that lasts forever. That is, if p_t is the equilibrium price for the asset, then

$$p_t + s_0 \prod_{r=0}^{T} (1 + r_\tau) \tag{37}$$

is also an equilibrium price, where s_0 is any positive constant. Under any hypothesis, however, *no* price that goes to infinity is a general equilibrium price, because families would then have infinite wealth in the limit, allowing additional consumption for at least one generation. In this way, speculative booms in nonreproducible assets can be ruled out.

Notes

1. The effect on the limit of family assets per person of one additional unit of consumption by generation t is

$$\lim_{T \to \infty} \left(\frac{1 + \rho(c)}{1 + n} \right)^{T-t} = 0.$$

References

D. Cass and M. Yaari. 1965. "Individual saving, aggregate capital accumulation, efficient growth," Cowles Foundation Discussion Paper No. 198, November 19.

P. A. Diamond. 1965. "The evaluation of infinite utility streams." *Econometrica* 33: 170–177.

P. A. Diamond. 1965. "National debt in a neoclassical growth model." *American Economic Review* 55: 1126–1150.

R. E. Hall. 1967. "Intertemporal preferences with variable rates of impatience."

E. S. Phelps. 1965. "Second essay on the golden rule." *American Economic Review* 55: 795–814.

P. S. Samuelson. 1958. "An exact consumption-loan model of interest." *Journal of Political Economy* 66: 467–482.

P. S. Samuelson. 1950. "The problem of integrability in utility theory." *Economica NS* 17: 355–385.

P. S. Samuelson. 1957. "A turnpike refutation of the golden rule in a welfare maximizing many-year plan." In K. Shell (ed.), *Essays in the Theory of Optimal Economic Growth*.

2 The Dynamic Effects of Fiscal Policy in an Economy with Foresight

This paper presents the results of a study of several related dynamic fiscal problems in a simple economic model whose distinguishing feature is that the participants in the economy are assumed to make plans by looking into the future. The competitive equilibrium in the presence of a changing fiscal policy is calculated and compared to the intertemporal equilibrium in the absence of any change. Throughout, we use the term equilibrium in its Walrasian sense, to indicate that all markets clear. In every case, we calculate the full general equilibrium in the economy, over all time periods and all markets. Part of the contribution of the paper, it is hoped, is in suggesting some methods for the characterization of intertemporal competitive equilibrium. Except for very general properties—existence of equilibrium and turnpike behavior—this area of study has received very little attention in the literature.

Since the actual calculation of the equilibrium is rather tediously algebraic, we have adopted the following organization: In section 2.1 we describe the model and indicate some of its properties. In section 2.2 we present, without proof, descriptions of the dynamic effects of a variety of fiscal policies. Finally, in section 2.3 we develop the analytic method applied in section 2.2.

Four fiscal policies are treated: a recurrent head tax, a consumption tax, an interest tax, and an investment credit. In almost every case, there are important anticipatory effects on the economy in advance of the imposition of the policy. Generally, the anticipatory effects help to smooth the jolt caused by the policy. For example, savings gradually increase in anticipation of the head tax, enabling individuals to maintain a smooth level of consumption in spite of the tax, although eventually consumption must be reduced by the whole amount of the tax. Even when the policy change causes a jolt in the real flows of the economy, as in the case of the consumption tax, the anticipatory effect is in the opposite direction to the jolt.

It is also instructive to note how the competitive price system acts to cushion the economy against the impact of a policy change. This is most strikingly illustrated in the case of the investment credit (defined as a negative excise tax on investment goods). In a partial equilibrium analysis ignoring the effect of the credit on interest rates, it appears that no rational

Reprinted with permission from *The Review of Economic Studies*, vol. 38 (2), April 1971, pp. 229–244.

entrepreneur would hold capital goods at the instant the credit became available. He could escape the capital loss induced by the credit, seemingly, by selling his capital goods just before the credit became available and buying them back an instant later. In fact, however, the simultaneous desire of all capital owners to sell and buy back causes a dramatic fall in the interest rate, excatly large enough to remove all the incentive to sell in the first place.

2.1 An Economy with Foresight

From the point of view of constructing a model in which today's equilibrium depends on future economic developments, consumers play the principal role. We suppose that there are a large number of identical individuals, each seeking to maximize an intertemporal utility function of the Ramsey form:

$$u(c_{-T},\ldots,c_0,\ldots,c_T) = \sum_{t=-T}^{T} \left(\frac{1}{1+\rho}\right)^t u(c_t). \tag{1}$$

Here c_t is the individual's consumption of the single consumption good assumed to be produced, ρ is his rate of impatience, assumed to be positive, and $u(\cdot)$ is an increasing, concave, twice-differentiable function. The economy exists only over the period from $-T$ to T; there is no population change over time. This is likely to be a good approximation to a more realistic model with partially overlapping generations if the life span is very long compared to the time scale of economic events.

Further, we assume that there is a credit market in which each individual can lend any amount between periods t and $t + 1$ at an interest rate r_t. Then to maximize utility, each individual will adjust his consumption plan to equate the marginal rate of substitution between consumption in any adjacent time periods to the price ratio as given by the interest rate:

$$\frac{u'(c_{t+1})/(1 + \rho)}{u'(c_t)} = \frac{1}{1 + r_t}. \tag{2}$$

Among all the consumption plans meeting this requirement, the most expensive one that can be financed by the consumer's wealth is chosen. The source of his wealth is discussed shortly.

On the producers' side, we simplify matters by assuming that there is only a single input to production called capital.[1] Gross output y_t is given by a twice-differentiable production function $f(k_t)$ with strictly decreasing returns to scale. We assume that consumption goods and capital goods are perfect substitutes in production, so there is no ambiguity in measuring gross output and capital goods in units of the consumption good. If a fraction δ of the capital stock has to be replaced each period, the following equation governs capital accumulation:

$$k_{t+1} = f(k_t) + (1 - \delta)k_t - c_{t+1}. \tag{3}$$

Note that consumption in period $t + 1$ comes out of the gross output of period t. We assume that all profits are distributed evenly among all the consumers: this is the source of consumers' wealth mentioned above. Now the interest rate in this economy can be shown by a simple arbitrage argument to equal the net marginal product of capital:

$$r_t = f'(k_t) - \delta. \tag{4}$$

We suppose that the economy begins with an endowment of resources $\bar{q}$ to be divided between immediate consumption and the initial capital stock k_{-T}. Finally, since no consumer will lend in period T, we require that k_T be zero.

If the aggregates in equation 3 are measured per capita, then the capital accumulation equation (equation 3) and the consumer marginal rate of substitution equation with the net marginal product of capital in place of the interest rate (equations 2 and 4), together with the initial and terminal conditions just mentioned, form a complete description of the competitive equilibrium:

$$k_{t+1} = f(k_t) + (1 + \delta)k_t - c_{t+1}, \tag{5}$$

$$u'(c_{t+1}) = \frac{1 + \rho}{1 + f'(k_t) - \delta} u'(c_t), \tag{6}$$

$$k_{-T} + c_{-T} = \bar{q}, \tag{7}$$

$$k_T = 0. \tag{8}$$

We note that any solution to this system of equations must be a general equilibrium: producer equilibrium is guaranteed by the equality of the interest rate and the net marginal product of capital. To show that consumers are in equilibrium, we observed that the marginal rate of substitution condition has already been imposed; it remains to show that the budget constraint is met exactly for each consumer. The latter can be established by the following argument: let A_t be a typical consumer's assets at time t. Then $A_{-T} = \bar{q} - c_{-T}$. One useful way to state the budget constraint is in the form that terminal assets be zero: $A_T = 0$. If π_t is the individual's share of profit and $r_t A_t$ is his interest income, his asset accumulation equation is

$$A_{t+1} = \pi_t + r_t A_t - c_{t+1}. \tag{9}$$

His share of profits is the difference between net output and interest payments, per capita:

$$\pi_t = f(k_t) - \delta k_t - r_t k_t. \tag{10}$$

Substituting this into the asset accumulation equation and comparing the result with the capital accumulation equation, we find that since $A_{-T} = k_{-T}$, they are equal in all periods, and, in particular, they are both zero in the last period, as required.

This establishes the equivalence between a solution to equations 5 through 8 and a competitive equilibrium. Existence and uniqueness of the equilibrium follow from general theorems of Debreu (1959) for existence and Arrow and Hurwicz (1958) for uniqueness. It is easily seen that the present model meets the hypotheses of these theorems.

Only a very limited characterization of the competitive equilibrium in this model will be given here, as the main results will be described in section 2.2 after the model has been extended to take account of fiscal action. In the first place, there is a unique stationary state in the model, say k^* and c^*, defined by

$$f'(k^*) - \delta = \rho \tag{11}$$

and

$$c^* = f(k^*) - \delta k^*. \tag{12}$$

That is, consumption remains stationary when the interest rate (the inducement to postpone consumption) is equal to the rate of impatience. The actual level of consumption is the net output produced by the capital stock held by producers at this interest rate. Second, the competitive equilibrium dispalys the turnpike property—even if k_{-T} is very low, k_t arches toward k^* before dropping to zero, and, in fact, tends to remain close to k^* for an increasing fraction of the time as T becomes larger. A formalization of this property and a proof for the differential equation version appear in Cass 1966.[2]

2.2   The Response to Fiscal Policy

In this section we describe the response of the economy to four different kinds of fiscal policy. In each case, there are no taxes for the period $-T$ through 0, and then one tax (or credit) is imposed suddenly beginning in period 1 and continuing until period T at the same rate. The fact that the policy will take effect in period 1 is known even in period $-T$. The four policies are (1) a recurrent head tax, (2) a consumption tax, (3) an interest tax, and (4) an investment credit.

In the discussion of the results it is assumed, implicitly, that the lifetime of the economy, $2T$, is long compared to the period in which there is a perceptible response to the policy. Futher, the actual length of a single period is assumed to be very short, so that the equilibrium will appear to be a smooth function of time, except in the cases where the policy induces a jump from period 0 to period 1.[3]

Existence and uniqueness of the competitive equilibrium in the model with taxes follow by obvious extensions of the results cited in the previous section. The important properties of the excess demand functions— continuity and satisfaction of the weak axiom of revealed preference—are unaffected by the introduction of a proportional gap between prices paid by consumers and prices received by producers.

We employ the following notation in describing the effects of the various policies under consideration:

λ_1 = positive characteristic root of the approximating linear system, as defined in section 2.3;

λ_2 = negative characteristic root;

A_c = departure of consumption from stationary level just before tax change; measures anticipatory effect. $A_c = c_0 - c^*$;

A_k = anticipatory effect on capital. $A_k = k_0 - k^*$;

J_c = jump in consumption induced by tax change. $J_c = c_1 - c_0$;

L_c = long-run departure of consumption from its stationary level.

$$L_c = \lim_{t \to \infty} c_t - c^*;$$

L_k = long-run departure of capital from its stationary level.

$$L_k = \lim_{t \to \infty} k_t - k^*.$$

In section 2.3 we show that to a good approximation, the path followed by the economy perturbed by a fully anticipated discrete change in fiscal policy is

$$\left. \begin{aligned} c_t &= c^* + A_c e^{\lambda_1 t} \\ k_t &= k^* + A_k e^{\lambda_1 t} \end{aligned} \right\} \quad t \leq 0 \tag{13} \tag{14}$$

$$\left. \begin{aligned} c_t &= c^* + L_c + (A_c + J_c - L_c)e^{\lambda_2 t} \\ k_t &= k^* + L_k + (A_k - L_k)e^{\lambda_2 t} \end{aligned} \right\} \quad t > 0. \tag{15} \tag{16}$$

Starting in the distant past at a point close to the stationary levels of consumption and capital, the economy follows an exponential path toward the point $c_0 = c^* + A_c$, $k_0 = k^* - A_k$ in anticipation of the policy change. The change itself may induce a jump in consumption.[4] After the jump, the economy follows an exponential path to a new stationary point, possibly differing from the old one because of permanent influences of the new taxes. Note that the response of the economy to perturbations is stable over time—$e^{\lambda_1 t}$ vanishes as t becomes large and negative and $e^{\lambda_2 t}$ vanishes as t becomes large and positive.

We begin with the case of a recurrent head tax requiring each taxpayer to pay a fixed quantity, γ_h, of goods to the government at the beginning of each period starting with period 1. In this and succeeding cases, we assume that the government disposes of the proceeds of the tax in a way that leaves consumers and producers unaffected. The anticipatory effects of the head tax are

$$A_c = \frac{\lambda_2}{\lambda_1 - \lambda_2} \gamma_h < 0, \tag{17}$$

$$A_k = \frac{1}{\lambda_1 - \lambda_2} \gamma_h > 0. \tag{18}$$

Consumption declines and capital rises in anticipation of the tax; this builds up a buffer stock of capital out of which the tax is paid initially. The quantity $-\lambda_2/\lambda_1 - \lambda_2$ lies between 0 and 1/2, so consumption declines by not some than half the amount of the tax.

No jump is induced by the head tax at the time of its imposition. In the competitive equilibrium, consumers pay the tax at first entirely out of accumulated wealth. As the capital stock is drawn down, however, more and more of the tax is paid by reducing consumption. In the long run, capital declines to its earlier stationary level, and consumption declines to a stationary level less than its earlier level by the full amount of the tax:

$$L_c = -\gamma_h, \tag{19}$$

$$L_k = 0. \tag{20}$$

To summarize the effects of the head tax, we give the expressions for the path of consumption:

$$c_t = c^* - \frac{-\lambda_2}{\lambda_1 - \lambda_2}\gamma_h e^{\lambda_1 t}, \qquad t \leqq 0,$$

$$= c^* - \left(1 - \frac{\lambda_1}{\lambda_1 - \lambda_2}e^{\lambda_2 t}\right)\gamma_h, \qquad t > 0. \tag{21}$$

Our second case is that of a consumption tax that raises the effective price of one unit of consumption to $1 + \gamma_c$ in period 1 and every succeeding period. The only substitution effect of this tax between adjacent periods is between c_0 and c_1, where it induces a downward jump in consumption. The general equilibrium accommodation to this jump affects consumption and capital in every period, but, in contrast to the head tax, the consumer is not cushioned against the jump itself.

To isolate the general equilibrium substitution effects of the consumption tax, we suppose first that it is combined with a negative head tax of equal yield. The anticipatory effects of this combination are

$$A_c = \frac{-\lambda_2}{\lambda_1 - \lambda_2}\frac{c^*}{E_c}\gamma_c > 0, \tag{22}$$

$$A_k = \frac{-1}{\lambda_1 - \lambda_2}\frac{c^*}{E_c}\gamma_c < 0, \tag{23}$$

where E_c is the absolute value of the elasticity of marginal utility with respect to consumption, evaluated at c^*:

$$E_c = -c^* \frac{u''(c^*)}{u'(c^*)}. \tag{24}$$

The jump in consumption is

$$J_c = -\frac{c^*}{E_c} \gamma_c < 0. \tag{25}$$

The anticipatory effect on consumption is no larger than one-half of the magnitude of the jump. With the compensating negative head tax, the consumption tax has no long-run effects. Thus as long as its rate is not changed, the consumption tax is perfectly neutral, in the sense that it has no substitution effect. But a fully anticipated change in the tax rate causes a serious jolt in the economy, one which the price system does not absorb, so the jolt appears in the real flows of the economy. Consumption rises and investment falls before the tax is imposed. At the moment of its imposition, consumption falls discontinuously and investment rises by the same amount. The capital stock and consumption gradually rise thereafter to their previous stationary values.

In the absence of the offsetting negative head tax, the response of the economy is similar, except that the anticipatory effect on consumption is smaller because of the opposite anticipatory effect of the income loss caused by the tax:

$$A_c = \frac{\lambda_2}{\lambda_1 - \lambda_2} \left(1 - \frac{1}{E_c} \right) c^* \gamma_c, \tag{26}$$

$$A_k = \frac{1}{\lambda_1 - \lambda_2} \left(1 - \frac{1}{E_c} \right) c^* \gamma_c. \tag{27}$$

If the elasticity of marginal utility is unity (for example, if $u(c) = \log c$), then the substitution and income effects exactly balance, and the economy gives no outward indication of its expectation of the policy change.

The consumption jump caused by the consumption tax is the same in the absence of the income offset as it was in the earlier case. The long-run effects without offset are

$$L_c = -c^* \gamma_c, \tag{28}$$

$$L_k = 0. \tag{29}$$

Our third case is that of an interest tax which reduces the effective rate of interest earned by consumers from $f'(k) - \delta$ to $(1 - \gamma_r)(f'(k) - \delta)$ for interest receipts in period 1 and every succeeding period. This might be imposed directly on consumers as a tax on interest income or on producers as a tax on capital earnings. The latter example is particularly interesting because it permits interpretation of our results as a dynamic theory of the shifting of the corporate income tax.

Once again we suppose that there is an offsetting negative head tax so that we can isolate the substitution effects of the tax. First, the anticipation effects are

$$A_c = \frac{\lambda_2^2}{\lambda_1 - \lambda_2} \frac{k^*}{E_k} \gamma_r > 0, \tag{30}$$

$$A_k = \frac{\lambda_2}{\lambda_1 - \lambda_2} \frac{k^*}{E_k} \gamma_r < 0. \tag{31}$$

E_k is the absolute value of the elasticity of the net marginal product of capital evaluated at the stationary level of capital:

$$E_k = -k^* \frac{f''(k^*)}{f'(k^*) - \delta}. \tag{32}$$

Consumption rises and capital falls in anticipation of the diminished return from capital after the tax. Significantly, no jump in either capital or consumption is induced by the sudden imposition of the tax. The capital stock continues its decline after the tax, and consumption begins to decline. Both approach levels in the long run that are lower than the earlier stationary levels:

$$L_c = -\rho \frac{k^*}{E_k} \gamma_r < 0, \tag{33}$$

$$L_k = -\frac{k^*}{E_k} \gamma_r < 0. \tag{34}$$

In spite of the income offset, long-run consumption is reduced by the substitution toward less capital caused by the interest tax. Compared to the consumption tax, the interest tax is better behaved in its impact effect but is costlier in the long run because of its permanent substitution effect.

If the interest tax is levied as a tax on capital earnings, it is natural to inquire into the extent to which the tax is shifted, that is, to what extent capital earnings per unit of capital increase to compensate for the tax. It is customary to define the rate of shifting, s, as the ratio of the amount of additional income before tax per unit of capital caused by the tax to the amount of tax per unit of capital if income were at the level that it would have been if there were no tax. In the present model,

$$s_t = \frac{f'(k_t) - \delta - \rho}{\rho \gamma_r}. \tag{35}$$

Using the linear approximation

$$f'(k_t) - \delta - \rho \doteq -(k_t - k^*) \frac{E_k}{k^*}, \tag{36}$$

we have

$$s_t = 1 - \frac{\lambda_1}{\lambda_1 - \lambda_2} e^{-\lambda_2 t}, \qquad t > 0. \tag{37}$$

Thus the rate of shifting starts at $-\lambda_2/\lambda_1 - \lambda_2$, which lies between 0 and 1/2, just after the tax is imposed and gradually approaches unity. This is in accord with the general belief that the rate of shifting in the short run is less than in the long run. It should be noted that this theory of shifting does not depend on the existence of short-run disequilibrium to explain the disparity between short- and long-run rates of shifting.

As a final case we consider an investment credit, which we take to be a negative excise tax at rate γ_k on investment goods, whether used for net investment or replacement. The investment credit has two distinct substitution effects. In the period that it first becomes available, it has the same substitution effect as a consumption tax at the equivalent rate, and, in fact, causes the same jump in consumption and investment. The credit also has a permanent substitution effect toward more capital, arising from its subsidy on replacement investment.

With an offsetting positive head tax the investment credit causes a response described by the following parameters:

$$A_c = \frac{\lambda_2}{\lambda_1 - \lambda_2} \left(\frac{c^*}{E_c} - \left(\left(\frac{\lambda_1}{\rho} - 1 \right) \frac{\rho + \delta}{E_k} \right) k^* \right) \gamma_k, \tag{38}$$

$$A_k = \frac{1}{\lambda_1 - \lambda_2}\left(\frac{c^*}{E_c} - \left(\left(\frac{\lambda_1}{\rho} - 1\right)\frac{\rho + \delta}{E_k}\right)k^*\right)\gamma_k, \tag{39}$$

$$J_c = -\frac{c^*}{E_c}\gamma_k < 0, \tag{40}$$

$$L_c = \frac{k^*}{E_k}(\rho + \delta)\gamma_k > 0, \tag{41}$$

$$L_k = \frac{\rho + \delta}{\rho}\frac{k^*}{E_k}\gamma_k > 0. \tag{42}$$

There are two opposing anticipation effects on consumption, a positive effect arising from the consumption tax aspect of the credit, and a negative effect arising from the negative interest tax aspect. In the long run, the investment credit increases both consumption and capital, at the cost of consumption foregone around the time of the initiation of the credit.

Although the investment credit induces a jump in the real flows in the economy, the price system does a great deal to cushion the economy against the shock. Effectively, the rate of interest becomes almost infinitely negative for loans between periods 0 and 1. If the interest rate remained constant, individual entrepreneurs would sell their capital in period 0 and but new capital with the benefit of the credit in period 1. In the competitive equilibrium, however, prices adjust to ensure that exactly the existing capital stock is held between periods 0 and 1.

2.3 Analytical Method

Our demonstration of the conclusions presented in the previous section proceeds in the following way. First, we develop an extended version of the model of equations 5 to 8. It differs from the earlier model in two respects: it incorporates parameters for the various tax policies that concern us, and it subdivides each time period into N subperiods. We then differentiate this model with respect to the tax parameters to get a system of equations describing the response of the competitive equilibrium to change. We evaluate this system along the stationary path and calcute the limit of the solution as the time span becomes large ($T \to \infty$) and the time interval becomes small ($N \to \infty$). We interpret the resulting expression as a linear approximation for finite changes in tax parameters, and this forms the basis for the conclusions of section 2.2. The validity of the approximation has been verified by explicit numerical calculation of the exact competitive equilibrium in a typical case for each policy.[5]

The complete model is the following:

$$u'(c_{j+1}) = \frac{1 + \dfrac{\rho}{N}}{1 + \dfrac{f'(k_j) - \delta}{N}} u'(c_j), \tag{43}$$

$$k_{j+1} = \frac{1}{N} f(k_j) + \left(1 + \frac{\delta}{N}\right) k_j - \frac{1}{N} c_{j+1}, \tag{44}$$

$\left.\right\} j < 0$

$$u'(c_1) = \frac{\left(1 + \dfrac{\rho}{N}\right)(1 + \theta_c)}{1 + (1 - \theta_r)\dfrac{f'(k_0) - \delta}{N} - \left(1 - \dfrac{\delta}{N}\right)\theta_k} u'(c_0), \tag{45}$$

$$k_1 = \left(1 - \frac{\delta}{N}\right) k_0 + \frac{1}{N}\frac{1}{1 - \theta_k}(f(k_0) - c_1 - \theta_h - \theta_c c_1)$$
$$- \theta_r(f'(k_0) - \delta)k_0), \tag{46}$$

$\left.\right\} j = 0$

$$u'(c_{j+1}) = \frac{\left(1 + \dfrac{\rho}{N}\right)(1 - \theta_k)}{1 + (1 - \theta_r)\dfrac{f'(k_j) - \delta}{N} - \left(1 - \dfrac{\delta}{N}\right)\theta_k} u'(c_j), \tag{47}$$

$$k_{j+1} = \left(1 - \frac{\delta}{N}\right) k_j + \frac{1}{N}\frac{1}{1 - \theta_k}(f(k_j) - c_{j+1} - \theta_h - \theta_c c_{j+1})$$
$$- \theta_r(f'(k_j) - \delta)k_j), \tag{48}$$

$\left.\right\} j > 0$

$$k_{-TN} + \frac{1}{N} c_{-TN} = k^* + \frac{1}{N} c^*, \tag{49}$$

$$k_{TN} = k^*. \tag{50}$$

The functions and parameters retain their definitions in terms of the original time units: for example, $1/N \, f(k)$ is the output produced in one subperiod with capital k. Note that the terminal condition, equation 50, differs from the more natural terminal condition of the previous section. This is purely for the sake of analytical convenience and has no effect on the results, since we consider only the limits as T and N become large. The tax parameters are defined as follows:

θ_h = amount of head, per capita per period,

θ_c = rate of consumption tax. The price, including tax, of one unit of consumption is $1 + \theta_c$,

θ_r = interest tax rate,

θ_k = rate of investment credit. The effective price of one unit of investment is $1 - \theta_k$.

To obtain a general expression for derivatives with respect to any of these parameters, we introduce dummy parameter, z, with the following relation to the θ's: $\theta_h = \gamma_h z$: $\theta_c = \gamma_c z$; $\theta_r = \gamma_r z$, and $\theta_k = \gamma_k z$. We calculate derivatives with respect to z and choose the γ's to represent one or another fiscal policy. This is especially convenient because the resulting expression in terms of the γ's can simply be reinterpreted as the linear approximation with the γ's serving as tax rates.

At this point we differentiate equations 42 to 49 with respect to z and evaluate the resulting system at the point $z = 0$, for which we know $c_j = c^*$ and $k_j = k^*$ for all j. If we let

$$
A(N) = \begin{bmatrix} 0 & -\dfrac{\rho}{1+\dfrac{\rho}{N}} \dfrac{c^* E_k}{E_c k^*} \\ -1 + \dfrac{1}{N} \dfrac{\rho}{1+\dfrac{\rho}{N}} \dfrac{c^* E_k}{E_c k^*} & \rho \end{bmatrix}, \tag{51}
$$

$$
S(N) = \begin{bmatrix} \dfrac{c^*}{E_c} \left(\gamma_c + \dfrac{1 - \dfrac{\delta}{N}}{1 + \dfrac{\rho}{N}} \gamma_k \right) \\ 0 \end{bmatrix}, \tag{52}
$$

$$b(N) = \begin{bmatrix} \dfrac{c^* \rho\gamma_r - (\rho + \delta)\gamma_k}{E_c} \\ 1 + \dfrac{\rho}{N} \\ -\gamma_h - c^*\gamma_c - \rho k^*\gamma_r + \delta k^*\gamma_k \end{bmatrix}, \tag{53}$$

$$x_j = \begin{bmatrix} \dfrac{dc_j}{dz} \\ \dfrac{dk_j}{dz} \end{bmatrix}, \tag{54}$$

then the resulting system is

$$x_{j+1} = \left(I + \frac{1}{N} A(N) \right) x, \qquad j < 0,$$

$$= \left(I + \frac{1}{N} A(N) \right) x_0 + \frac{1}{N} b(N) + S(N), \qquad j = 0,$$

$$= \left(I + \frac{1}{N} A(N) \right) x_j + \frac{1}{N} b(N), \qquad j > 0; \tag{55}$$

$$\frac{1}{N} x_{1,-TN} + x_{2,-TN} = 0, \tag{56}$$

$$x_{2,TN} = 0. \tag{57}$$

Here I is a 2×2 identity matrix.

The vector $S(N)$ gives the structural shock associated with the consumption tax and the investment credit, and the vector $b(N)$ gives the permanent structural effects of the various taxes; the first element contains substitution effects of the interest tax and investment credit and the second element, income effects of all the taxes. The problem at this point is to calculate the reduced form or solution of this set of structural equations. Since the system is linear with constant coefficients, there is no obstacle in principle to solving it directly. A great simplification is achieved, however, by calculating the limit of the solution as the time span becomes large (to eliminate end effects) and as the time interval becomes short (to eliminate nuisance terms that arise from the use of discrete time). Nothing of economic interest is lost by taking this limit.[6]

In the appendix it is shown that the limiting solution to system of this kind has the following form:

$$x(t) = M_0 e^{\lambda_1 t} \begin{bmatrix} \lambda_2 \\ 1 \end{bmatrix}, \qquad t \leq 0,$$

$$= M_1 e^{\lambda_2 t} \begin{bmatrix} \lambda_1 \\ 1 \end{bmatrix} + \begin{bmatrix} m_1 \\ m_2 \end{bmatrix}, \qquad t > 0, \tag{58}$$

where λ_1 and λ_2 are characteristic roots of $A = \lim_{N \to \infty} A(N)$; $M_0, M_1, m_1,$ and m_2 are constants depending on $b = \lim_{N \to \infty} b(N)$; and $S = \lim_{N \to \infty} S(N)$ in the following way:

$$\begin{bmatrix} m_1 \\ m_2 \end{bmatrix} = -A^{-1} b. \tag{59}$$

$$M_0 = \frac{S_1 - \lambda_1 S_2 - m_1 + \lambda_1 m_2}{\lambda_1 - \lambda_2}, \tag{60}$$

$$M_1 = \frac{S_1 - \lambda_1 S_2 - m_1 + \lambda_2 m_2}{\lambda_1 + \lambda_2}. \tag{61}$$

In the present case,

$$A = \begin{bmatrix} 0 & -\rho \dfrac{c^* E_k}{E_c k^*} \\ -1 & \rho \end{bmatrix}, \tag{62}$$

$$S = \begin{bmatrix} \dfrac{c^*}{E_c} (\gamma_c + \gamma_k) \\ 0 \end{bmatrix}, \tag{63}$$

$$b = \begin{bmatrix} \dfrac{c^*}{E_c} (\rho \gamma_r - (\rho + \delta) \gamma_k) \\ -\gamma_h - c^* \gamma_c - \rho k^* \gamma_r + \delta k^* \gamma_k \end{bmatrix}. \tag{64}$$

The characteristic roots of A are

$$\lambda_1 = \frac{\rho + \left(\rho^2 + 4\rho \dfrac{c^* E_k}{E_c k^*} \right)^{1/2}}{2} > 0, \tag{65}$$

$$\lambda_2 = \frac{\rho - \left(\rho^2 + 4\rho \dfrac{c^* E_k}{E_c k^*}\right)^{1/2}}{2} < 0. \tag{66}$$

Thus the long-run effects are

$$L_c = m_1 = \frac{k^*}{E_k}(\rho\gamma_r - (\rho + \delta)\gamma_k) - \gamma_h - c^*\gamma_c - \rho k^*\gamma_r + \delta k^*\gamma_k, \tag{67}$$

$$L_k = m_2 = \frac{1}{\rho}\frac{k^*}{E_k}(\rho\gamma_r - (\rho + \delta)\gamma_k). \tag{68}$$

The general anticipatory effects are

$$A_k = M_0 = \frac{1}{\lambda_1 - \lambda_2}\left(\gamma_h + \left(\frac{1}{E_c} + 1\right)c^*\gamma_c + \left(\rho - \frac{\lambda_2}{E_k}\right)k^*\right)\gamma_r$$

$$+ \left(\frac{c^*}{E_c} - \left(\left(\frac{\lambda_1}{\rho} - 1\right)\frac{\rho + \delta}{E_k} + \delta\right)k^*\right)\gamma_k \tag{69}$$

and

$$A_c = \lambda_2 M_0. \tag{70}$$

Finally,

$$J_c = S_1 = -\frac{c^*}{E_c}(\gamma_c + \gamma_k). \tag{71}$$

Next, we note how these results are used to obtain a linear approximation to the true competitive equilibrium with a particular fiscal policy. In general, the true equilibrium can be written

$$x_t = \bar{x}_t(\theta_h, \theta_c, \theta_r, \theta_k). \tag{72}$$

In each of these depends on the dummy parameter, z, then a linear approximation to x_t is

$$x_t \doteq \bar{x}_t(0, 0, 0, 0) + \left(\frac{\partial \bar{x}_t}{\partial \theta_h}\frac{d\theta_h}{dz} + \frac{\partial \bar{x}_t}{\partial \theta_c}\frac{d\theta_c}{dz} + \frac{\partial \bar{x}_t}{\partial \theta_r}\frac{d\theta_r}{dz} + \frac{\partial \bar{x}_t}{\partial \theta_k}\frac{d\theta_k}{dz}\right)z, \tag{73}$$

or

$$x_t \doteq \begin{bmatrix} c^* \\ k^* \end{bmatrix} + \left(\frac{\partial \bar{x}_t}{\partial \theta_h}\gamma_h + \cdots + \frac{\partial \bar{x}_t}{\partial \theta_k}\gamma_k\right)z. \tag{74}$$

The expression inside the parentheses is exactly what we have derived above. By setting $z = 1$, we see that this expression itself serves as a linear approximation to the departure from the stationary state if each γ is interpreted as a tax rate itself.

The various policies studied are defined as follows

1. Head tax: $\gamma_h > 0$; $\gamma_c = \gamma_r = \gamma_k = 0$.

2a. Consumption tax, with income offset: $\gamma_c > 0$; $\gamma_h = -c^*\gamma_c$; $\gamma_r = \gamma_k = 0$.

  b. Consumption tax, no offset: $\gamma_c > 0$, $\gamma_h = \gamma_r = \gamma_k = 0$.

3. Interest tax, income offset: $\gamma_r > 0$, $\gamma_h = -\rho k^*\gamma_r$, $\gamma_c = \gamma_k = 0$.

4. Investment credit, income offset: $\gamma_k > 0$, $\gamma_h = \delta k^*\gamma_k$, $\gamma_c = \gamma_r = 0$.

Appendix

LEMMA. *Suppose*

$$x_{j+1} = \left(I + \frac{1}{N}A(N)\right)x_j, \qquad 0 \leq j \leq TN - 1, \tag{A1}$$

$$\hat{\beta}_1(N)x_{1,TN} + \beta_2(N)x_{2,TN} = 0, \tag{A2}$$

where x_j is a two-dimensional vector:

$$x_j = \begin{bmatrix} x_{1,j} \\ x_{2,j} \end{bmatrix}, \tag{A3}$$

I is a 2×2 identity matrix, and $A(N)$ is a 2×2 matrix with properties

$$\lim_{N \to \infty} A(N) = A = \begin{bmatrix} 0 & a_{12} \\ a_{21} & a_{22} \end{bmatrix}, \tag{A4}$$

$$a_{12}a_{21} > 0, \tag{A5}$$

$$a_{22} > 0. \tag{A6}$$

Suppose further that

$$\lim_{N \to \infty} \beta_1(N) = \beta_1, \tag{A7}$$

$$\lim_{N \to \infty} \beta_2(N) = \beta_2, \tag{A8}$$

and that one of the two functions $\beta_1(N)$ and $\beta_2(N)$ is nonzero for all N. Then

$$\lim_{N\to\infty} \lim_{T\to\infty} x_{[Nt]} = e^{\lambda_2 t}\begin{bmatrix}\lambda_1\\1\end{bmatrix}x_{2,0} \tag{A9}$$

for all $t \geqq 0$ and all $x_{2,0}$.

$[Nt]$ *is the greatest integer less than Nt and λ_2 is the negative character-istic root of A.*

Proof. We note first that the characteristics roots of A are real and opposite in sign: $\lambda_1 > 0$ and $\lambda_2 < 0$, and that the corresponding characteristic vectors can be written

$$\begin{bmatrix}\lambda_2\\1\end{bmatrix}\text{ and }\begin{bmatrix}\lambda_1\\1\end{bmatrix}. \tag{A10}$$

Now let $L(N)$ be the diagonal matrix of characteristic roots of $I + 1/N$ $A(N)$:

$$L(N) = \begin{bmatrix}1 + \dfrac{1}{N}\lambda_1(N) & 0\\[2ex] 0 & 1 + \dfrac{1}{N}\lambda_2(N)\end{bmatrix} \tag{A11}$$

and let $H(N)$ be a matrix of characteristic vectors of $I + 1/N$ $A(N)$ (these are also characteristic vectors of $A(N)$ itself). It is easily seen by direct calculation that

$$\lim_{N\to\infty} \lambda_1(N) = \lambda_1, \tag{A12}$$

$$\lim_{N\to\infty} \lambda_2(N) = \lambda_2, \tag{A13}$$

and that there is a sequence of normalizations of $H(N)$ such that

$$\lim_{N\to\infty} H(N) = \begin{bmatrix}\lambda_2 & \lambda_2\\1 & 1\end{bmatrix}. \tag{A14}$$

At least for suitably large values of N, $\lambda_1(N) > 0$, $\lambda_2(N) < 0$, and $H(N)$ admits the normalization

$$H(N) = \begin{bmatrix}h_1(N) & h_2(N)\\1 & 1\end{bmatrix}. \tag{A15}$$

Hence forth we restrict our attention to values of N large enough for these to hold.

The solution to the difference equation stated in terms of these matrices is

$$x_j = H(N)(L(N))^j(H(N))^{-1}x_0. \tag{A16}$$

Substituting the terminal conditions and writing the equation in terms of the matrix elements, we find

$$
\begin{aligned}
0 = \frac{1}{h_1(N) - h_2(N)} \Bigg\{ &\Bigg[\beta_1(N)\left\{ h_1(N)\left(1 + \frac{\lambda_1(N)}{N}\right)TN \right. \\
&- h_2(N)\left(1 + \frac{\lambda_1(N)}{N}\right)TN \Bigg\} + \beta_2(N)\left\{\left(1 + \frac{\lambda_1(N)}{N}\right)TN \right. \\
&- \left(1 + \frac{\lambda_2(N)}{N}\right)TN \Bigg\} \Bigg]x_{1,0} + \Bigg[\beta_1(N)h_1(N)h_2(N)\left\{-\left(1 + \frac{\lambda_1(N)}{N}\right)TN \right. \\
&+ \left(1 + \frac{\lambda_2(N)}{N}\right)TN \Bigg\} + \beta_2(N)\left\{-h_2(N)\left(1 + \frac{\lambda_1(N)}{N}\right)TN \right. \\
&+ h_1(N)\left(1 + \frac{\lambda_2(N)}{N}\right)TN \Bigg\} \Bigg]x_{2,0} \Bigg\}.
\end{aligned}
\tag{A17}
$$

Solving this for $x_{1,0}$ and taking the limit as $T \to \infty$, we find that the terms with

$$\left(1 + \frac{\lambda_1(N)}{N}\right)TN$$

predominate, giving

$$\lim_{T \to \infty} x_{1,0} = h_2(N)x_{2,0}. \tag{A18}$$

Thus for an arbitrary period, j, the solution has the property

$$\lim_{T \to \infty} x_j = \left(1 + \frac{\lambda_2(N)}{N}\right)^j \begin{bmatrix} h_2(N) \\ 1 \end{bmatrix} x_{2,0}. \tag{A19}$$

Finally, we consider $j = [Nt]$ for an arbitrary t:

$$\left(1 + \frac{\lambda_2(N)}{N}\right)^{[Nt]} = \left(1 + \frac{\lambda_2(N)}{N}\right)^{Nt}\left(1 + \frac{\lambda_2(N)}{N}\right)^{[Nt] - Nt}. \tag{A20}$$

Now

$$\lim_{N \to \infty} \left(1 + \frac{\lambda_2(N)}{N}\right)[Nt]$$

$$= \left(\lim_{N \to \infty} \left(1 + \frac{\lambda_2(N)}{N}\right)Nt\right)\left(\lim_{N \to \infty} \left(1 + \frac{\lambda_2(N)}{N}\right)[Nt] - Nt\right)$$

$$= e^{\lambda_2 t}. \tag{A21}$$

We conclude that

$$\lim_{N \to \infty} \lim_{T \to \infty} x_{[Nt]} = e^{\lambda_2 t} \begin{bmatrix} \lambda_1 \\ 1 \end{bmatrix} x_{2,0} \tag{A22}$$

as required.

THEOREM. *Suppose*

$$x_{j+1} = \left(I + \frac{1}{N} A(N)\right)x_j, \qquad j = -TN, \dots, -1, \tag{A23}$$

$$x_1 = \left(I + \frac{1}{N} A(N)\right)x_0 + \frac{1}{N} b(N) + S(N), \tag{A24}$$

$$x_{j+1} = \left(I + \frac{1}{N} A(N)\right)x_j + \frac{1}{N} b(N), \qquad j = 1, \dots, TN - 1, \tag{A25}$$

$$\frac{1}{N} x_{1,-TN} + x_{2,-TN} = 0. \tag{A26}$$

$$x_{2,TN} = 0. \tag{A27}$$

where x_j, I, and $A(N)$ are as defined in the lemma, and $b(N)$ and $S(N)$ are two-dimensional vectors with limits as follows:

$$\lim_{N \to \infty} b(N) = b, \tag{A28}$$

$$\lim_{N \to \infty} S(N) = S. \tag{A29}$$

Then

$$\lim_{N \to \infty} \lim_{T \to \infty} x_{[Nt]} = M_0 e^{\lambda_1 t} \begin{bmatrix} \lambda_2 \\ 1 \end{bmatrix}, \qquad t \leqq 0,$$

$$= M_1 e^{\lambda_2 t} \begin{bmatrix} \lambda_1 \\ 1 \end{bmatrix} + \begin{bmatrix} m_1 \\ m_2 \end{bmatrix}, \qquad t > 0, \tag{A30}$$

where M_0, M_1, m_1, and m_2 are constants depending on A, b, and S in the following way:

$$\begin{bmatrix} m_1 \\ m_2 \end{bmatrix} = -A^{-1}b, \tag{A31}$$

$$M_0 = \frac{S_1 - \lambda_1 S_2 + \lambda_1 m_2 - m_1}{\lambda_1 - \lambda_2}, \tag{A32}$$

$$M_1 = \frac{S_1 - \lambda_1 S_2 + \lambda_2 m_2 - m_1}{\lambda_1 - \lambda_2}, \tag{A33}$$

Proof. The proof consists of a double application of the lemma. For $j < 0$, we can write the difference equation with time reversed:

$$x_{k+1} = \left(I + \frac{1}{N} A(N)\right)^{-1} x_k, \qquad k > 0$$

$$= \left(I + \frac{1}{N} B(N)\right) x_k. \tag{A34}$$

The matrix $B(N)$ so defined is easily seen to have the following property:

$$\lim_{N \to \infty} B(N) = -A. \tag{A35}$$

Further, its characteristic roots are $-\lambda_1$ and $-\lambda_2$, and its matrix of characteristic vectors is H. Thus we have, as $N \to \infty$ and $T \to \infty$,

$$x_{1,0} = \lambda_2 x_{2,0} \tag{A36}$$

by the previous lemma.

For $j > 0$, we need to take account of the inhomogeneity of the difference equation. For this purpose, we define

$$y_j = x_j + \frac{1}{N}(A(N))^{-1}b(n). \tag{A37}$$

Then

$$y_{j+1} = \left(I + \frac{1}{N} A(N)\right) y_j, \tag{A38}$$

and a suitable application of our earlier result gives, as $N \to \infty$ and $T \to \infty$,

$$y_{1,1} = \lambda_1 y_{2,1}. \tag{A39}$$

In terms of $x_{1,1}$ and $x_{2,1}$, this can be written

$$x_{1,1} = (\lambda_1\alpha_{21} - \alpha_{11})b_1 + (\lambda_1\alpha_{22} - \alpha_{12})b_2 + \lambda_1 x_{2,1}, \tag{A40}$$

where

$$\begin{bmatrix} \alpha_{11} & \alpha_{12} \\ \alpha_{21} & \alpha_{22} \end{bmatrix} = A^{-1}. \tag{A41}$$

At $j = 0$, we have, as $N \to \infty$

$$x_{1,1} = x_{1,0} + S_1, \tag{A42}$$

$$x_{2,1} = x_{2,0} + S_2, \tag{A43}$$

This gives a linear system of four equations in the four variables $x_{1,0}$, $x_{2,0}$, $x_{1,1}$, and $x_{2,1}$. If we let

$$\begin{bmatrix} m_1 \\ m_2 \end{bmatrix} = -A^{-1}b, \tag{A44}$$

we can write its solution as follows:

$$x_{1,0} = \lambda_2 \frac{S_1 - \lambda_1 S_2 + \lambda_1 m_2 - m_1}{\lambda_1 - \lambda_2}, \tag{A45}$$

$$x_{2,0} = \frac{x_{1,0}}{\lambda_2}, \tag{A46}$$

$$x_{1,1} = \lambda_1 \frac{S_1 - \lambda_2 S_2 + \lambda_2 m_2 - m_1}{\lambda_1 - \lambda_2} + m_1, \tag{A47}$$

$$x_{2,1} = \frac{S_1 - \lambda_2 S_2 + \lambda_2 m_2 - m_1}{\lambda_1 - \lambda_2} + m_2. \tag{A48}$$

Finally, the expression for the limiting solution for arbitrary t given in the lemma can be applied to derive the expression for the solution appearing in the statement of the theorem.

Notes

1. The results would remain unchanged if inelastically supplied labor also entered as an input.

2. Cass treats the formally equivalent problem of optimal growth with a Ramsey social welfare function.

3. In an earlier draft, the intellectually more satisfactory case of continuous time and an infinite lifetime was treated. This introduced a number of deep but essentially spurious difficulties, which, although not insoluble, could only obscure the main points of the paper.

4. Policies other than the ones discussed here could induce a jump in the capital stock. This could be incorporated by defining a parameter J_k. An example of such a policy is a capital levy.

5. The author is grateful to Michael Hurd for programming these calculations.

6. It would be even simpler to calculate the solution to the limit of the system of equations rather than the limit to the solution. Unfortunately the first limit does not exist, because of the shock term $S(N)$. This is the source of the difficulty mentioned in note 3.

References

Arrow, K. J., and Hurwicz, L. 1958. "On the Stability of Competitive Equilibrium, I." *Econometrica* 26, 522–552.

Cass, D. 1966. "Optimum Growth in an Aggregative Model of Capital Accumulation: A Turnpike Theorem." *Econometrica* 34, 833–850.

Debreu, G. 1959. *The Theory of Value*, Cowles Foundation Monograph 17 (New York, Wiley).

3 Consumption Taxes versus Income Taxes: Implications for Economic Growth

The prevalence of tax systems whose yield exceeds a quarter or even a third of national income suggests that the study of the global economic implications of alternative taxes should have high priority. In fact, this is not the case. The study of the global effects of taxes has been largely confined to the area of stabilization, where it has reached a high degree of sophistication.[1] Relatively little attention has been paid to the following kind of question: What would happen, in the long run, if the federal income tax were replaced by a federal sales tax that maintained the same level of aggregate demand? This is a distinctly non-Keynesian question, since its answer is trivial in a simple Keynesian model. My purpose here is to focus on this question as representative of the many questions that could be asked about the global implications of alternative tax systems. In the course of this I will present a new interpretation of an important non-Keynesian model of economic equilibrium.

The difference between an income tax and a consumption tax is exactly the taxation of savings under the former but not under the latter. For this reason, most of my concern here is with the development of a theory of saving that can be applied to this problem. The actual application is quite straightforward and yields a surprisingly definite answer. We focus on the savings-consumption decision rather than the labor-leisure decision, not because the second is any less important, but because it is the first that is inherently intertemporal. Furthermore, there are no sharp differences in the effects of the two taxes on the labor-leisure choice, whereas the differences are striking for consumption and saving.

A single example is carried through the entire paper. Although the parameters of the model in the example were estimated in the most casual way, it is still intended to suggest the orders of magnitude of the equilibrium values of the variables involved.

3.1 A Theory of Saving Appropriate for the Comparison of Taxes

The starting point for this investigation is the well-known life-cycle hypothesis of Modigliani and his collaborators.[2] The important characteristic of this theory is that individuals save for a purpose, namely future consumption. It is crucially important that a model of savings behavior for our

Reprinted with permission from the National Tax Association, *Proceedings of the 61st National Tax Conference*, San Francisco, September 2–6, 1968.

purpose take account of the motivation for savings, since the difference between the two taxes is in their treatment of savings. The analysis of the influence of taxes involves an examination of the reactions of savers to changes in the payoff to savings; this can be done can with an explicit examination of their motivation. Thus the simple Keynesian rule-of-thumb savings hypothesis, so useful in problems of stabilization, would be inappropriate here.[3]

In its simplest form, Modigliani's hypothesis holds that consumers allocate their total human and material wealth over the years of their lifetimes in constant proportions.[4] More precisely, the present value, say at age 21, of consumption at any future age is a fixed fraction of total wealth at age 21; this fraction is independent of many market variables. It is natural to assume that consumers are impatient, so that the share of wealth going to consumption in early years is larger than that going to later years. This does not mean that consumption is less in later years; the wealth set aside at the beginning of the plan appreciates at the rate of interest until the consumption takes place. For convenience, we assume a fixed rate of impatience. Then if the rate of interest happens exactly to equal the rate of impatience, the consumption plan has equal consumption in all years of the individual's life, while if the rate of interest exceeds the rate of impatience, planned consumption will rise over the individual's lifetime. In both cases, the amount of wealth allocated to successive years' consumption declines over the lifetime.

It will be useful later to have this hypothesis formulated in algebraic terms. If c_t is the consumption of a representative individual in the tth year of his life, W is his wealth measured at $t = 1$ (again, this might actually be age 21), r is the interest rate, and ρ is the rate of impatience, then the constant proportions hypothesis is

$$\frac{\left(\frac{1}{1+r}\right)^{t-1} c_t}{c_1} = \left(\frac{1}{1+\rho}\right)^{t-1}. \tag{1}$$

Here the expression $[1/(1 + r)]^{t-1} c_t$ is the amount of wealth set aside for future consumption in year t; compound interest at rate r will cause it to increase to c_t by that year.

The overall allocation of wealth is governed by a wealth budget constraint. In the absence of inheritance and bequests, the individual is constrained to spend exactly his total wealth over his lifetime; that is, the present value of his planned consumption must equal his total wealth:

$$W = c_1 + \left(\frac{1}{1+r}\right)c_2 + \left(\frac{1}{1+r}\right)^2 c_3 + \cdots + \left(\frac{1}{1+r}\right)^{T-1} c_T, \qquad (2)$$

for the individual with a life expectancy of T years. From equation 1 this can be written in terms of first-year consumption, c_1:

$$W = c_1 + \left(\frac{1}{1+\rho}\right)c_2 + \left(\frac{1}{1+r}\right)^2 c_3 + \cdots + \left(\frac{1}{1+r}\right)^{T-1} c_1, \qquad (3)$$

Thus first-year consumption is given by

$$c_1 = \frac{W}{1 + \dfrac{1}{1+\rho} + \left(\dfrac{1}{1+\rho}\right)^2 + \cdots + \left(\dfrac{1}{1+\rho}\right)^{T-1}} \qquad (4)$$

$$= \frac{W}{G_T\left(\dfrac{1}{1+\rho}\right)};$$

here we have introduced a shorthand notation for the sum of a finite geometric series. The function $G_T(\cdot)$ is defined as $G_T(X) = 1 + X + X^2 + \cdots + X^{T-1} = 1/(1-X)(1-X^T)$. $G_T(1/(1+\rho))$ can be thought of as the present value of a unit stream of income lasting from the present until year T, evaluated at interest rate ρ.

The fact that the interest rate does not appear in equation 4 establishes the following proposition: For a given level of total wealth, W, first-year consumption, c_1, is utterly insensitive to changes in the interest rate. This seems to suggest that the hope expressed at the beginning of this section that the life-cycle model can distinguish between consumption and income taxes is wholly illusory; if the interest rate does not affect consumption behavior in this model, how can the model predict different responses to taxes which differ only in their treatment of savings?

The answer to this question leads naturally into the discussion of the aggregative implications of the life-cycle hypothesis. Two comments should be made immediately. First, although for given values of W, c_1 is unaffected by changes in r, the same is not true for $c_2, \ldots, c_T$. The higher the interest rate, the higher is the value of the wealth set aside for consumption in years after the first. Thus the interest rate sensitivity of future consumption is positive and becomes larger as more distant consumption is considered.

Second, it is misleading to take wealth as fixed when considering changes in the interest rate. A youth in the first period of his life has nothing but human wealth (the present value of his future wages) when he makes his consumption plan. The higher the interest rate, the lower is the present value of these wages. Futher, under reasonable assumptions about the production side of the economy, there is an inverse relation between wages and the interest rate. This also causes W to drop when r rises. Taken together, these qualifications suggest that the overall interest rate sensitivity of an individual's consumption plan is negative at the outset and rises to a positive value for the last few years of the plan.

In order to obtain an exact aggregate view of the interest rate sensitivity of consumption and saving, it is necessary to add up the consumption levels for all of the generations alive during any one year.[5] Under the assumption that the population grows at a constant annual rate (say, n), there are always more younger people than older people in the population. Since younger people have negative interest rate sensitivity, this suggests that the higher the rate of population growth, the lower (or more negative) is the interest rate response of aggregate (steady-state) consumption. The interesting and important conclusion of the examination of the interest rate sensitivity of aggregate is that for small rates of population growth and long lifetimes, this sensitivity can become indefinitely large even when the sensitivity of c_1 given W is zero. This fact was been overlooked in the theoretical literature on savings and consumption; its recognition makes possible a reconciliation of two divergent branches of that literature.[6] The relationship between the steady-state level of aggregate consumption and the interest rate is shown in a diagram in figure 3.1.

Aggregate consumption reaches its minimum at an interest rate midway between the rate of growth of the population and the rate of impatience (throughout it is assumed that ρ exceeds n). At interest rate near ρ, consumption responds positively to increases in the interest rate. In this region, the consumption plan of each individual calls for roughly equal consumption in each year of his life. But one of the consequences of the fact that high powers of $(1 + r)/(1 + \rho)$ determine consumption in later years is that this consumption has a higher sensitivity to changes in the interest rate. Consumption in early years does not share this sensitivity. On the other hand, the income effect of increases in the interest rate is communicated proportionally to all years in the consumption plan. Thus at high interest

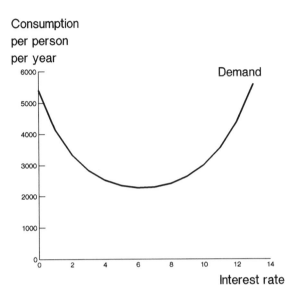

Figure 3.1
Steady-state consumption demand as a function of the interest rate

rates, the large positive response of consumers in the later years of their lives dominates the response of aggregate consumption to changes in the interest rate, and the curve in figure 3.1 slopes upward.

For low interest rates, however, consumption plans decline over each individual's lifetime. Most consumption is done by younger people with negative interest rate sensitivity, so the aggregate consumption curve slopes downward in this region. If this sounds somewhat farfetched, it is reassuring to note that the general equilibrium theory presented in the next section predicts that the steady-state interest rate will lie in the neighborhood of the rate of impatience, where consumers behave normally.

All these assertions require support in terms of the algebra of the model. The first step is to derive a formula for aggregate consumption per capita given the consumption plan followed by consumers. If the population is growing at the constant rate, n, then at any time a fraction $(1 + n)^{T-1}/ G_T(1 + n)$ of the population comprises people in the first year of their consumption plans, a fraction $(1 + n)^{T-2}/G_T(1 + n)$ comprises people in the second year, and so forth. These provide the appropriate weights for adding up $c_1, \ldots, c_t$ to get aggregate consumption per capita:

$$c = \frac{(1+n)^{T-1}}{G_T(1+n)}c_1 + \frac{(1+n)^{T-2}}{G_T(1+n)}c_2 + \cdots + \frac{1}{G_T(1+n)}c_T. \tag{5}$$

Now the constant proportions hypothesis expressed in equation 1 can be invoked to get c in terms of c_1 and the interest rate:

$$c = \frac{(1+n)^{T-1}}{G_T(1+n)}c_1 + \frac{(1+n)^{T-2}}{G_T(1+n)}\frac{1+r}{1+\rho}c_1 + \cdots$$

$$+ \frac{1}{G_T(1+n)}\left(\frac{1+r}{1+\rho}\right)^{T-1}c_1. \tag{6}$$

The next step is to substitute for c_1 its expression in terms of wealth from equation 4:

$$c = \frac{W(1+n)^{T-1}}{G_T\left(\dfrac{1}{1+\rho}\right)G_T(1+n)}\left[1 + \left(\frac{1+r}{(1+n)(1+\rho)}\right)\right.$$

$$\left. + \left(\frac{1+r}{(1+n)(1+\rho)}\right)^2 + \cdots + \left(\frac{1+r}{(1+n)(1+\rho)}\right)^{T-1}\right] \tag{7}$$

Now

$$\frac{(1+n)^{T-1}}{G_T(1+n)} = \frac{1}{G_T\left(\dfrac{1}{1+n}\right)};$$

inserting this and applying the G_T function to the summation inside the brackets gives

$$c = W\frac{G_T\left(\dfrac{1+r}{(1+n)(1+\rho)}\right)}{G_T\left(\dfrac{1}{1+\rho}\right)G_T\left(\dfrac{1}{1+n}\right)}. \tag{8}$$

Were it not for the dependence of wealth, W, on the interest rate, equation 8 would describe the curve shown in figure 3.1. The last step in setting down the algebra of the life-cycle hypothesis is to state explicitly the form of this dependence.

In the absence of inheritance, wealth at the beginning of any individual's career is purely human wealth—that is, the present value of future earnings.

Under the simplifying assumption that in the steady state, all individuals receive the same wage, w, individual initial wealth W is

$$W = wG_T\left(\frac{1}{1+r}\right). \tag{9}$$

This relationship could be modified to take account of two salient characteristics of lifetime earnings ignored here: the tendency for earnings to rise over an individual's lifetime, and the tendency for people to spend a significant portion of their lifetimes on retirement.[7]

Finally, the description of the relationship between steady-state consumption and the interest rate can be completed by observing that there is a systematic inverse relationship between the steady-state wage and the steady-state interest rate; this can be written

$$w = \phi(r). \tag{10}$$

Collecting these results together gives the algebraic expression for the curve in figure 3.1:

$$c = \phi(r)\frac{G_T\left(\dfrac{1}{1+r}\right)G_T\left(\dfrac{1+r}{(1+n)(1+\rho)}\right)}{G_T\left(\dfrac{1}{1+\rho}\right)G_T\left(\dfrac{1}{1+n}\right)}. \tag{11}$$

At two interest rates this formula has a simple form; these are $r = n$ and $r = \rho$, where $c = \phi(n)$ and $c = \phi(\rho)$, respectively. That is, at these interest rates, steady-state consumption per person is exactly equal to the wage— all wages are consumed and all property income is saved. Between these interest rates, consumption is less than the wage and net saving is even higher. At interest rates higher than the rate of impatience,

$$G_T\left(\frac{1+r}{(1+n)(1+\rho)}\right)$$

begins to rise rapidly, especially if $1 + r$ exceeds $(1 + n)(1 + \rho)$, since in that region it is the sum of a *divergent* geometric series. Similarly, $G_T(1/(1 + r))$ rises rapidly as the interest rate approaches zero, for the same reason. The first of these effects is the mathematical embodiment of the observation made earlier that at high interest rates, the positive interest sensitivity of older generations dominates the aggregate response of consumption to the interest rate. The second demonstrates that at low interest rates, the negative effect on wealth of increasing interest rates dominates the response of aggregate consumption.

Exactly how responsive to changes in the interest rate is aggregate consumption? Figure 3.1 is drawn with the following assumptions: rate of impatience, $\rho = 0.10$, rate of population growth, $n = 0.015$, wages as a function of the interest rate, $\phi(r) = \$1500/\sqrt{r + 0.15}$ per man-year (the form of this function will be justified shortly), lifetime, $T = 70$ years. These are intended to approximate the contemporary American economy. Figure 3.1 suggests that if the life-cycle hypothesis holds, aggregate consumption is quite sensitive, indeed, to the interest rate. For example, if the interest rate were to rise by one percentage point, from 0.10 to 0.11, consumption per person per year would rise by close to 20%, from \$3000 to \$3560. Thus the traditional conclusion, that the interest response of the consumption of a utility-maximizing individual can be either positive or negative but is sure to be small, cannot possibly be carried over to the case of aggregate consumption and a realistic lifetime. In the latter case, for the relevant range of interest rates (slightly above the rate of impatience), aggregate consumption rises very steeply with the interest rate.

So far we have dealt with consumers' intertemporal decisions in terms of the resulting aggregate consumption. The analysis can also be stated in terms of aggregate asset accumulation. High interest rate sensitivity of consumption turns out to imply high sensitivity of aggregate asset holdings.

Now with a low interest rate, impatience causes individuals to consume more in the early years of their lives than in the late years. This early consumption is financed by borrowing against future earnings. The result is that each consumer is always in debt; his indebtedness reaches a peak around middle age and then declines, reaching zero at his death. Consequently, aggregate asset holdings of consumers are always negative if the rate of interest is less than the rate of impatience. If the interest rate is exactly equal to the rate of impatience, consumers neither save nor dissave, and aggregate assets are zero. Finally, in the realistic case where the interest rate exceeds the rate of impatience, consumers accumulate assets in the early parts of their careers in anticipation of higher consumption in later years. Whenever r exceeds ρ, aggregate asset holdings are positive.

These conclusions could be supported in terms of the algebra of the life-cycle model, by finding individual asset holdings as a function of age and aggregating by the age distribution of the population, exactly as was done above for consumption. Fortunately, this is made unnecessary by the availability of an easy shortcut. If steady-state consumption is different from the wage, the difference must be accounted for by interest receipts on asset holdings. This relation can be turned on its head to give asset holdings in terms of aggregate consumption; we already know how the latter is related to the interest rate.

In the steady rate, assets per person are the same in one year as they were in the previous year. Now what remains of last year's assets is $(1 + r) A + w - c$, where A denotes assets per person. But this year there are $1 + n$ people for each person last year. Thus the relation among these variables that defines the steady state is

$$A = \frac{(1 + r)A + w - c}{1 + n}. \tag{12}$$

Solving this for A and substituting $\phi(r)$ for w gives

$$A = \frac{c(r) - \phi(r)}{r - n}. \tag{13}$$

By $c(r)$ we mean the consumption demand function shown in figure 3.1. If the interest rate is less than the rate or population growth, the numerator

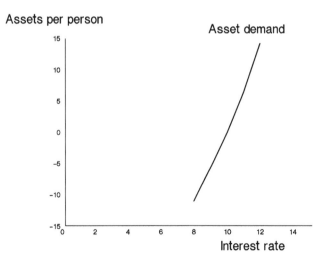

Figure 3.2
Asset demand per person as a function of the interest rate

of equation 13 is positive and the denominator is negative. If the interest rate lies between n and ρ, the numerator is negative and the denominator is positive. In both cases, aggregate assets are negative. Finally, if r exceeds ρ, both the numerator and denominator are positive, and aggregate assets are positive. This establishes the assertions made above. In figure 3.2 we present the relation between assets per person and the interest rate implied by the curve in figure 3.1.

3.2   General Equilibrium with Life-cycle Savings

We assume that the standard one-sector growth model technology prevails. Net output per person, y, depends on capital per person, k, according to a production function with diminishing returns to capital, $y = f(k)$. Capital deterioration is accounted for in $f(k)$, so the interest rate will equal the net marginal product of capital, $r - f'(k)$, provided credit markets are competitive. Steady states in this technology are achieved when the part of output not consumed is exactly large enough to equip next year's large labor force with the same amount of capital as this year's. Combinations of steady-state levels of consumption and the interest rate meeting this requirement form the curve shown in figure 3.3. At high interest rates, there is a capital shortage, and steady-state consumption is low. At low interest rates, the capital stock per person is so large that most output is devoted to equipping new workers. The maximum point on this curve is at an interest rate equal to the rate of growth of the population; this is the familiar theorem of the golden rule.

The production function used in drawing figure 3.3 is a Cobb-Douglas function with capital share $1/3$ and 15% of capital input lost as deterioration:

$$y = f(k) = 248k^{1/3} - 0.15k. \tag{14}$$

Some facts about this function are useful to set down. First, the interest rate corresponding to a level, k, of capital stock per person is

$$r = f'(k) = k^{-2/3} - 0.15. \tag{15}$$

Conversely, the amount of capital per person can be calculated from the inverse of equation 15:

$$k = \left(\frac{r + 0.15}{83}\right)^{-3/2} \tag{16}$$

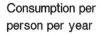

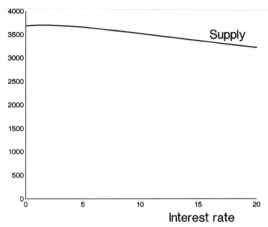

Figure 3.3
Steady-state consumption supply as a function of the interest rate in the one-sector technology

The wage can be calculated most easily from the fact that factor shares of gross ouput are constant for a Cobb-Douglas production function:

$$w = 165k^{1/3}. \tag{17}$$

Our $\phi(r)$ function is obtained by substituting the formula for k in terms of r from equation 16:

$$w = \phi(r) = 1500(r + 0.15)^{-1/2}. \tag{18}$$

Armed with these results, we can look at steady-state general equilibrium in two equivalent ways. First, in a graph with consumption on the vertical axis and the interest rate on the horizontal axis, we can find the equilibrium as the intersection of the consumption demand curve implied by the life-cycle savings hypothesis and the supply curve defined the technology. Equivalently, we can put capital and assets on the vertical axis and the interest rate again on the horizontal axis; then the equilibrium lies at the intersection of the asset demand curve and the marginal product curve and gives the relation between capital stock and the interest rate. The logic of the second view is that in equilibrium, the demand for assets must equal

Consumption per
person per year

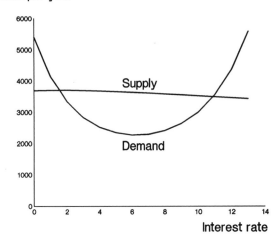

Assets, capital
per person

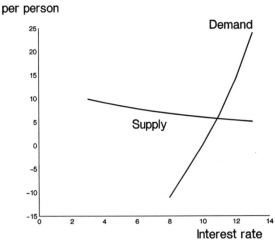

Figure 3.4
Alternative views of steady-state equilibrium in the life-cycle savings model

the capital stock, since there is no other way to hold wealth in this economy. These two views are illustrated in figure 3.4.

On the top of figure 3.4 there is a second intersection at $r = n$ in addition to the expected one at $r > \rho$. Is it possible for this economy to have a steady-state equilibrium at the golden rule? Here we have a failure (in a sense) of the intertemporal form of Walras' law—clearing of the output market does not imply clearing of the capital market, since there is no corresponding intersection in the right-hand side of figure 3.4. The precise reason for this anomaly need not detain us here; the curious reader should consult Cass and Yaari (1967) for an explanation. The capital market diagram makes it clear that the golden rule cannot be a steady-state equilibrium in the life-cycle model.

3.3   Taxes in the Life-cycle Model of Intertemporal Equilibrium

A proportional consumption tax[8] can be illustrated most easily on the consumption–interest rate diagram. If the vertical axis is taken to be the actual amount of consumption (as opposed to consumption expenditures, which exceed consumption by the amount of the tax), then the effect of the tax on the steady-state consumption demand curve is to shift it downward proportionally, so that the level of consumption expenditures after the tax is the same, at any interest rate, as the level of consumption before the tax. This follows from the observation that a rational consumer, faced with a proportional tax on consumption, allocates consumption *expenditures* over his lifetime in precisely the same way that he would allocate consumption in the absence of the tax.[9]

On the supply side, we need to derive a supply function that is net of government purchases, since these represent a diversion from consumption. Our assumption is that government purchases are a constant fraction (equal to the tax rate) of the total supply to final demand at any interest rate. This assumption guarantees that the government budget is balanced no matter where the equilibrium falls; it could be replaced without affecting the analysis by any other assumption about government expenditures that resulted in a balanced budget at the particular interest rate characteristic of equilibrium. To be perfectly rigorous, we must also require that neither production nor consumption activities be affected by governmet expenditures—military expenditures are the archetype in our view of government purchases. Under these assumptions, the supply curve shifts downward proportionally, so that at any interest rate, the net supply after the imposition of a consumption tax and corresponding expenditure program is less than supply in the absence of the expenditures by the amount of the consumption tax yield.

These supply and demand curves are shown in figure 3.5. Since both curves shift downward by the same proportion, the after-tax steady-state equilibrium occurs at exactly the same interest rate as the before-tax equilibrium. This establishes the well-known proposition that a consumption tax is intertemporally neutral in the sense that total output is unaffected by the tax and expenditure program—there is no deadweight loss associated with a consumption tax.

This neutrality is not shared by the income tax. As we shall see, total output is reduced by the imposition of an income tax (and balanced-budget expenditure policy); the reduction in consumption exceeds the yield of the tax. This defect of the income tax led Irving Fisher, and later Nicholas Kaldor (1955), to very forceful support of consumption taxes to replace income taxes. The argument of the present paper supports the claims of the proponents of a consumption tax in that the general equilibrium analysis

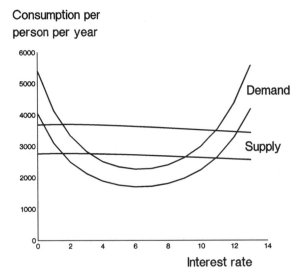

Figure 3.5
Effect of a 33% tax on consumption in the economy of figure 3.4 (upper intersection represents the economy in the absence of the tax; lower represents it with the tax)

confirms their basically partial equilibrium criticism of the income tax. On the other hand, our results suggest that the magnitude of the deadweight loss from an income tax is hardly large enough to cause serious concern.

An income tax has two effects on the life-cycle behavior of consumers. Like the consumption tax, it reduces demand proportionally at equivalent interest rates because of the need to pay the tax. But unlike the consumption tax, the income tax causes the consumer to use a lower interest rate in his consumption planning than the producer uses in his planning. Herein lies the source of the inefficiency of the income tax. It is the familiar double taxation of savings inherent in a tax falling on both wages and interest receipts that accounts for the deadweight loss.

If we continue to put the interest rate paid by producers to their consumer-bondholders on the horizontal axis of the supply-and-demand diagram, then we must look to the left on the before-tax diagram to find consumption demand after taxes, since the corresponding after-tax interest rate is proportionally lower. Thus the demand curve after taxes will lie proportionally to the *right* of the before-tax curve, as well as below it. Since the demand curve slopes upward quite steeply, it is practially guaranteed that the after-tax interest rate will exceed the before-tax rate by an amount close to the tax rate. In a sense, the question of the effect of the income tax on the interest rate is the same as the question of the shifting of the corporate income tax, in that one way of imposing an income tax is as a combination of a corporate profits tax (assuming all businesses are corporations) and a wage tax.[10] The life-cycle model gives a rather definite answer to the shifting question—the interest rate rises almost enough in the presence of an income tax to maintain the after-tax interest rate at its previous level. That is, tax shifting is close to 100% in this model.

An assumption about government expenditures that parallels our assumption in the consumption tax case is the following: at any interest rate, government expenditures are set equal to the yield of the income tax at the level of income generated by the technology at that interest rate. Again, this assumption is made for convenience in drawing the graphs; the analysis would remain unchanged for any program of government expenditures which had the same level at the equilibrium interest rate.

Supply-and-demand curves for the case of an income tax of 25% are shown in figure 3.6. The new steady-state interest rate is 14.3%, compared to 10.9% in the absence of the tax, implying a rate of shifting of 98.3%. Consumption drops from $3487 to $2533 per person per year after the

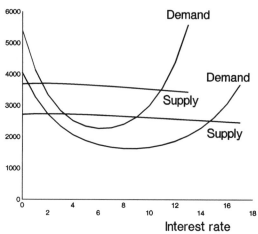

Figure 3.6
Effect of a 25% income tax on the economy of figure 3.4 (upper intersection represents the economy in the absence of the tax; lower represents it with the tax)

imposition of the tax. The yield of the tax (and level of government expenditures) is $862 per person per year, so the deadweight loss associated with a 25% income tax is $3487 − ($2533 + $862) = $92 per person per year. By contrast, the 33% consumption tax yields $872 per person per year and permits consumption of $2615 per person per year.

Thus we see that the dramatic effects of an income tax are largely confined to a substantial increment in the interest rate. Compared to a neutral alternative source of government revenue (the consumption tax), the income tax is more than 97% efficient in its effect on consumption. What accounts for its good performance? The potentially harmful effect of the income tax is in driving a wedge between consumers' and producers' interest rates. In the diagram this is seen as the deflection of the consumption demand curve to the right. The consequences of this deflection depend on the downward slope of the supply function; if it is steep, it is costly to the economy to have the interest rate driven up. But under realistic assumptions about production, the supply curve turns out to be practically flat. This is basically a consequence of the relatively small share that capital actually has in production. If capital were a more important factor, then the cost of inefficiency in its accumulation would be larger. As it happens, however, the case for a consumption tax over an income tax cannot be made very forcefully on the grounds of efficiency in savings and investment.

3.4 Implications for Economic Growth

In the long run, the rate of growth of the economy is the subject of purely technological determination. Without technical progress, the steady-state rate of growth of output cannot exceed the rate of growth of the population. In view of this limitation, the very long run effects on the rate of economic growth of alternative tax systems are all the same. But this is by no means the end of the story. As we have seen, different taxes imply different *levels* of economic activity. Any change in the tax system that takes the economy to a new steady-state level causes a temporary (but possibly rather long-lasting) change in the growth rate.

Thus if the federal government were to switch to a sales tax in place of the personal income tax, our analysis would suggest that the rate of growth would be higher for a few years, allowing consumption to rise to make up for the deadweight loss of the current income tax. Calculations based on a dynamic model not presented here indicate that the adjustment rate is high enough to close two-thirds of the gap within 5 years or so.[11] It is unlikely, however, that the growth would register in any but the most sensitive economic indicator. An overall change in output of 3%, distributed over several years, would hardly be noticeable in an economy whose movements are not otherwise particularly smooth.

On the other hand, this policy change would have conspicuous effects on economic variables other than output. The interest rate would decline by essentially the full amount of the tax, in reflection of the more generous treatment of savings under a consumption tax. As a result, investment would be stimulated during the period of transition, until the marginal product of capital was driven down to the new lower interest rate. More investment requires more saving, which in turn implies a *lower* level of consumption, at least at the beginning of the transition. A higher steady-state level of consumption is obtained only by sacrificing consumption at the beginning of the program. Tax reform, just like any other program to bring about growth by stimulating investment, has an immediate cost as well as a long-run benefit.

Our conclusion can hardly be other than that the argument from economic efficiency for a consumption tax is weak indeed. A careful examination of the life-cycle model of intertemporal equilibrium has shown that while there is an inefficiency associated with an income tax, its steady-state value is quite small and can be escaped only by a temporary further reduction in consumption.

Having stated the conclusions (and, in fact, the whole analysis) in rather a bold fashion, we are obligated to discuss some of the qualifications that necessarily attach to this kind of economics. We shall be particularly concerned with qualifications that suggest a weakening of our conclusions in the sense that they suggest a greater loss associated with a nonneutral tax like the income tax.

The assumption of our model that largely determines our conclusions is that the supply curve for steady-state consumption is almost flat. It would be more steeply downward-sloped if either the elasticity of output with respect to capital were larger, or if substitutibility between capital and labor were larger. On both counts our assumptions were generous. One-third is surely an outside estimate for the elasticity of gross output with respect to capital. The unitary elasticity of substitution of the Cobb-Douglas production function also seems about as high as economists are likely to agree upon.

The substantive conclusion for the present purpose emerging from the study of the life-cycle savings hypothesis is that the steady-state demand curve for consumption as a function of the interest rate is upward-sloping (though possibly very steep). The fact that it cannot slope downward limits the rate of shifting of the interest tax component of the income tax to 100% or less and thereby limits the interest rate response to a value less than or equal to the tax rate. Do the realistic qualifications to an admittedly rather stylized model suggest that the demand curve might slope downward? Among the most important of these qualifications is that people lack the predictive ability to make lifetime plans of the kind described in the model. But the principal hypothesis underlying our conclusion that the demand curve slopes upward is that the consumption level of the typical individual rises over his lifetime and that the interest sensitivity of older people should be greater than that of younger people (in our usual sense of the comparison of steady states). The first of these is likely to withstand almost any attempt to make the theory more realistic, since it is a matter of empirical fact. The second is more debatable; presumably the effect of uncertainty and other complications is to reduce interest sensitivity of people of all ages. As a first approximation, however, it seems unlikely that they might cancel out the formidable influence of interest compounded over the length of a lifetime. Furthermore, we should be cautious about overstating the degree and influence of uncertainty in what is predominantly a middle-class society. Uncertainty about future income is surely greater than uncertainty about how wealth should be spread over a lifetime, yet it is the latter which is important for our conclusion.

Notes

I am indebted to Peter Diamond and Franco Modigliani for useful suggestions at an early stage in my work on this subject. This research was supported by the Office of Emergency Planning.

1. For example, in the second Brookings Model volume (Fromm and Taubman 1968).

2. See Modigliani and Brumberg (1955), Modigliani (1961), and Ando and Modigliani (1963). Irving Fisher is generally thought to have been the first to suggest this approach to intertemporal equilibrium. Two excellent presentations of the life-cycle model within the context of contemporary mathematical growth theory are those of Cass and Yaari (1967) and Tobin (1967). The present exposition follows these rather closely, differing mainly in its emphasis.

3. This is not intended to imply that Keynes himself was not concerned with the influence of interest rates on savings. Rather, the thinking of Keynes and his successors (notably Patinkin) was confined to an individual savings function depending on income and the interest rate which could be blown up to get an aggregate savings function of the same form. Modigliani's key contribution (in this author's interpretation) was to point out that the individual savings function depends in an important way on the age of the individual and that consequently the aggregate savings function could have a very different form than that of any individual savings function. The development of this view (which is the principal novel feature of this paper) is the main burden of this first section.

4. This is equivalent to maximizing a Cobb-Douglas intertemporal utility function; on this, see Thompson (1967).

5. This assumes that consumption plans are actually fulfilled. They are sure to be fulfilled if the economy is in a steady state. From this point forward, comparisons are always between steady states.

6. Modigliani (1961), Samuelson (1958), Diamond (1965), and Cass and Yaari (1967) have studied intertemporal equilibrium with short lifetimes and have emphasized the anomalies that may arise there. Sidrauski (1967), Shell and Stiglitz (1967), and many others have studied models in which people effectively live forever and have noted their favorable or optimal aspects.

7. This is done with considerable care in the previously cited study of Tobin (1967).

8. By which we mean an expenditures tax, a sales tax on consumption goods, or a value-added tax with a deduction for investment expenditures.

9. A rigorous justification of this assertion would require an appeal to the foundation of the life-cycle hypothesis in intertemporal utility maximization.

10. The empirical literature on tax shifting has concentrated almost exclusively on the supply side of the capital market. Some caution is called for an comparing the idea of tax shifting mentioned here in the context of a model with perfect markets and the usual idea of tax shifting as a characteristic of highly imperfect markets.

11. The dynamic model, but not the calculations, appears in Hall (1967).

References

Albert Ando and Franco Modigliani. 1963. "The Life Cycle Hypothesis of Saving." *American Economic Review*, 53 (March): 55–84; "The Life Cycle Hypothesis of Saving: Correction." *American Economic Review* 54 (March): 111–113.

David Cass and Menahem Yaari. 1967. "Individual Savings, Aggregate Capital Accumulation, and Efficient Growth." In Karl Shell (ed.), *Essays on the Theory of Optimal Economic Growth* (Cambridge: MIT Press), pp. 233–268.

Peter A. Diamond. 1965. "National Debt in a Neoclassical Growth Model." *American Economic Review* 55: 1126–1150.

Gary Fromm and Paul Taubman. 1968. *Policy Simulations with an Econometric Model* (Washington, D.C.: Brookings Institution).

Robert E. Hall. 1967. "The Dynamic Effects of Fiscal Policy in an Economy with Foresight. Working Paper #119, Institute for Business and Economic Research, University of California, Berkeley, November (chapter 2 in this volume).

Nicholas Kaldor. 1955. *An Expenditure Tax* (London: George Allen and Unwin).

Franco Modigliani. 1967. "Long-run Implications of Alternative Fiscal Policies and the Burden of the National Debt." *Economic Journal* 71 (December): 730–755.

Franco Modigliani and Albert Ando. 1960. "The 'Permanent Income' and 'Life Cycle' Hypothesis of Saving Behavior: Comparison and Tests." In *Proceedings of the Conference on Consumption and Saving*, Vol. 2 (Philadelphia).

Franco Modigliani and Richard Brumberg. 1955. "Utility Analysis and the Consumption Function: An Interpretation of Cross-Section Data." In K. K. Kurihara (ed.), *Post-Keynesian Economics* (London: George Allen and Unwin).

Paul A. Samuelson. 1958. *Journal of Political Economy*.

Karl Shell and Joseph E. Stiglitz. 1967. "The Allocation of Investment in a Dynamic Economy," *Quarterly Journal of Economics* 81 (November): 592–609.

Miguel Sidrauski. 1967. "A Theory of Economic Growth in a Monetary Economy," unpublished mimco.

Earl A. Thompson. 1967. "Intertemporal Utility Functions and the Long Run Consumption Function." *Econometrica* 35 (April): 356–361.

James Tobin. 1967. "Life Cycle Saving and Balanced Growth." In *Ten Economic Studied in the Tradition of Irving Fisher* (New York: John Wiley & Sons).

II CONSUMPTION UNDER UNCERTAINTY

4 Stochastic Implications of the Life Cycle–Permanent Income Hypothesis: Theory and Evidence

Optimization of the part of consumers is shown to imply that the marginal utility of consumption evolves according to a random walk with trend. To a reasonable approximation, consumption itself should evolve in the same way. In particular, no variable apart from current consumption should be of any value in predicting future consumption. This implication is tested with time-series data for the postwar United States. It is confirmed for real disposable income, which has no predictive power for consumption, but rejected for an index of stock prices. The paper concludes that the evidence supports a modified version of the life cycle–permanent income hypothesis.

As a matter of theory, the life-cycle–permanent income hypothesis is widely accepted as the proper application of the theory of the consumer to the problem of dividing consumption between the present and the future. According to the hypothesis, consumers form estimates of their ability to consume in the long run and then set current consumption to the appropriate fraction of that estimate. The estimate may be stated in the form of wealth, following Modigliani, in which case the fraction is the annuity value of wealth, or as permanent income, following Friedman, in which case the fraction should be very close to one. The major problem in empirical research based on the hypothesis has arisen in fitting the part of the model that relates current and past observed income to expected future income. The relationship almost always takes the form of a fixed distributed lag, though this practice has been very effectively criticized by Robert Lucas (1976). Further, the estimated distributed lag is usually puzzlingly short. Equations purporting to embody the life-cycle–permanent income principle are actually little different from the simple Keynesian consumption function where consumption is determined by contemporaneous income alone.

Much empirical research is seriously weakened by failing to take proper account of the endogeneity of income when it is the major independent variable in the consumption function. Classic papers by Haavelmo (1943) and Friedman and Becker (1957) showed clearly how the practice of treating income as exogenous in a consumption function severely distorts the estimated function. Even so, regressions with consumption as the dependent variable continue to be estimated and interpreted within the life cycle–permanent income framework.[1]

Reprinted with permission from *Journal of Political Economy*, vol. 86, no. 6, pp. 971–987, © 1978 by the University of Chicago.

Though, in principle, simultaneous-equations econometric techniques can be used to estimate the structural consumption function when is major right-hand variable is endogenous, these techniques rest on the hypothesis that certain observed variables, used as instruments, are truly exogenous yet have an important influence on income. The two requirements are often contradictory, and estimation is based on an uneasy compromise where the exogeneity of the instruments is uncertain. Furthermore, the hypothesis of exogeneity is untestable.

This paper takes an alternative econometric approach to the study of the life-cycle–permanent income hypothesis by asking exactly what can be learned from a consumption regression where it is conceded from the outset that none of the right-hand variables is exogenous. This proceeds from a theoretical examination of the stochastic implications of the theory. When consumers maximize expected future utility, it is shown that the conditional expectation of future marginal utility is a function of today's level of consumption alone—all other information is irrelevant. In other words, apart from a trend, marginal utility obeys a random walk. If marginal utility is a linear function of consumption, then the implied stochastic properties of consumption are also those of a random walk, again apart from a trend. Regression techniques can always reveal the conditional expectation of consumption or marginal utility given past consumption and any other past variables. The strong stochastic implication of the life-cycle–permanent income hypothesis is that only consumption lagged one period should have a nonzero coefficient in such a regression. This implication can be tested rigorously without any assumptions about exogeneity.

Testing of the theoretical implication proceeds as follows: The simplest implication of the hypothesis is that consumption lagged more than one period has no predictive power for current consumption. A more stringent testable implication of the random-walk hypothesis holds that consumption is unrelated to *any* economic variable that is observed in earlier periods. In particular, lagged income should have no explanatory power with respect to consumption. Previous research on consumption has suggested that lagged income might be a good predictor of current consumption, but this hypothesis is inconsistent with the intelligent, forward-looking behavior of consumers that forms the basis of the permanent-income theory. If the previous value of consumption incorporated all information about the well-being of consumers at that time, then lagged values of actual income should have no additional explanatory value once lagged consumption is included. The data support this view—lagged income has a slightly negative coefficient in an equation with consumption as the dependent variable and lagged consumption as an independent variable. Of course, contemporaneous income has high explanatory value, but this does not contradict the principal stochastic implication of the life-cycle–permanent income hypothesis.

As a final test of the random-walk hypothesis, the predictive power of lagged values of corporate stock prices is tested. Changes in stock prices lagged by a single quarter are found to have a measurable value in predicting changes in consumption, which in a formal sense refutes the simple random-walk hypothesis. However, the finding is consistent with a modification of the hypothesis that recognizes a brief lag between changes in permanent income and the corresponding changes in consumption. The discovery that consumption moves in a way similar to stock prices actually supports this modification of the random-walk hypothesis, since stock prices are well known to obey a random walk themselves.

The paper concludes with a discussion of the implications of the pure life-cycle–permanent income hypothesis for macroeconomic forecasting and policy analysis. If every deviation of consumption from its trend is unexpected and permanent, then the best forecast of future consumption is just today's level adjusted for trend. Forecasts of future changes in income are irrelevant, since the information used in preparing them is already incorporated in today's consumption. In a forecasting model, consumption should be treated as an exogenous variable. For policy analysis, the pure life cycle–permanent income hypothesis supports the modern view that only unexpected changes in policy affect consumption—everything known about future changes in policy is already incorporated in present consumption. Further, unexpected changes in policy affect consumption only to the extent that they affect permanent income, and then their effects are expected to be permanent. Policies that have a transitory effect on income are incapable of having a transitory effect on consumption. However, none of the findings of the paper imply that policies affecting income have no effect on consumption. For example, a permanent tax reduction generates an immediate increase in permanent income and thus an immediate increase in consumption. But the evidence that policies act only through permanent income certainly complicates the problem of formulating countercyclical policies that act through consumption.

4.1 Theory

Consider the conventional model of life-cycle consumption under uncertainty: maximize $E_t \sum_{\tau=0}^{T-t}(1 + \delta)^{-\tau}u(c_{t+\tau})$ subject to $\sum_{\tau=0}^{T-t}(1 + r)^{-\tau}(c_{t+\tau} - w_{t+\tau}) = A_t$. The notation used throughout the paper is as follows:

E_t = mathematical expectation conditional on all
     information available in t;

δ = rate of subjective time preference;

r = real rate of interest ($r \geqq \delta$), assumed constant over time;

T = length of economic life;

$u()$ = one-period utility function, strictly concave;

c_t = consumption;

w_t = earnings;

A_t = assets apart from human capital.

Earnings, w_t, are stochastic and are the only source of uncertainty. In each period, t, the consumer chooses consumption, c_t, to maximize expected lifetime utility in the light of all information available then. The consumer knows the value of w_t when choosing c_t. No specific assumptions are made about the stochastic properties of w_t except that the conditional expectation of future earnings given today's information, $E_t w_{t+\tau}$, exists. In particular, successive w_t's are not assumed to be independent, nor is w_t required to be stationary in any sense.[2]

The principal theoretical result, proved in the appendix, is the following:

THEOREM. Suppose the consumer maximizes expected utility, as stated previously. Then $E_t u'(c_{t+1}) = [(1 + \delta)/(1 + r)]u'(c_t)$.

The implications of this result are presented in a series of corollaries.

COROLLARY 1. No information available in period t apart from the level of consumption, c_t, helps predict future consumption, c_{t+1}, in the sense of affecting the expected value of marginal utility. In particular, income or wealth in periods t or earlier is irrelevant, once c_t is known.

COROLLARY 2. Marginal utility obeys the regression relation, $u'(c_{t+1}) = \gamma u'(c_t) + \varepsilon_{t+1}$, where $\gamma = (1 + \delta)/(1 + r)$ and ε_{t+1} is a true regression disturbance; that is, $E_t \varepsilon_{t+1} = 0$.

COROLLARY 3. If the utility function is quadratic, $u(c_t) = -\frac{1}{2}(\bar{c} - c_t)^2$ (where $\bar{c}$ is the bliss level of consumption), then consumption obeys the exact regression, $c_{t+1} = \beta_0 + \gamma c_t - \varepsilon_{t+1}$, with $\beta_0 = \bar{c}(r - \delta)/(1 + r)$. Again, no variable observed in period t or earlier will have a nonzero coefficient if added to this regression.

COROLLARY 4. If the utility function has the constant elasticity of substitution form, $u(c_t) = c_t^{(\sigma-1)/\sigma}$, then the following statistical model describes the evolution of consumption: $c_{t+1}^{-1/\sigma} = \gamma c_t^{-1/\sigma} + \varepsilon_{t+1}$.

COROLLARY 5. Suppose that the change in marginal utility from one period to the next is small, both because the interest rate is close to the rate of time preference and because the stochastic change is small. Then consumption itself obeys a random walk, apart from trend.[3] Specifically, $c_{t+1} = \lambda_t c_t + \varepsilon_{t+1}/u''(c_t) + $ higher-order terms, where λ_t is $[(1 + \delta)/(1 + r)]$ raised to the power of the reciprocal of the elasticity of marginal utility

$$\lambda_t = \left(\frac{1 + \delta}{1 + r}\right)^{u'(c_t)/c_t u''(c_t)}$$

The rate of growth, λ_t, exceeds 1 because u'' is negative. It may change over time if the elasticity of marginal utility depends on the level of consumption. However, it seems likely that constancy of λ_t will be a good approximation, at least over a decade or two. Further, the factor $1/u''(c_t)$ in the disturbance is of little concern in regression work—it might introduce a mild heteroscedasticity, but it would not bias the results of ordinary least squares. From this point on, ε_t will be redefined to incorporate $1/u''(c_t)$ where appropriate.

This line of reasoning reaches the conclusion that the simple relationship $c_t = \lambda c_{t-1} + \varepsilon_t$ where ε_t is unpredictable at time $t - 1$, is a close approximation to the stochastic behavior of consumption under the life cycle—permanent income hypothesis. The disturbance, ε_t, summarizes the impact of all new information that becomes available in period t about the consumer's lifetime well-being. Its relation to other economic variables can be seen in the following way. First, assets, A_t, evolve according to $A_t = (1 + r)(A_{t-1} - c_{t-1} + w_{t-1})$. Second, let H_t be human capital, defined as current earnings plus the expected present value of future earnings: $H_t = \sum_{\tau=0}^{T-t}(1+r)^{-\tau}E_t w_{t+\tau}$, where H_t evolves according to $H_t = (1+r)(H_{t-1} - w_{t-1}) + \sum_{\tau=0}^{T-t}(1+r)^{-\tau}(E_t w_{t+\tau} - E_{t-1}w_{t+\tau})$. Let η_t be the second term, that is, the present value of the set of changes in expectations of future earnings that occur between $t-1$ and t. Then by construction, $E_{t-1}\eta_t = 0$. Still, the first term in the expression for H_t may introduce a complicated inter-temporal dependence into its stochastic behavior; only under very special circumstances will it be a random walk. The implied stochastic equation for total wealth is $A_t + H_t = (1+r)(A_{t-1} + H_{t-1} - c_{t-1}) + \eta_t$. The evolution of total wealth then depends on the relationship between the new information about wealth, η_t, and the induced change in consumption as measured by ε_t. Under certainty equivalence, justified either by quadratic utility or by the small size of ε_t, the relationship is simple: $\varepsilon_t = [1 + \lambda/(1+r) + \cdots + \lambda^{T-t}/(1+r)^{T-t}]\eta_t = \alpha_t \eta_t$. This is the modified annuity value of the increment in wealth. The modification takes account of the consumer's plans to make consumption grow at proportional rate λ over the rest of his life. Then the stochastic equation for total wealth is $A_t + H_t = (1+r)(1 - \alpha_{t-1})(A_{t-1} + H_{t-1}) + \eta_t$, which is a random walk with trend.

Consumers, then, process all available information each period about current and future earnings. They convert data on earnings, which may have large, predictable movements over time, into human capital, which evolves according to a combination of a highly predictable element associated with the realization of current earnings and an unpredictable element associated with changing expectations about future earnings. Taking account as well of financial assets accumulated from past earnings, consumers determine an appropriate current level of consumption. As shown at the beginning of this section, this implies that marginal utility evolves as a random walk with trend. As a result of consumers's optimization, wealth also evolves as a random walk with trend. Although it is tempting to summarize the theory by saying that consumption is proportional to wealth, wealth is a random walk, and so consumption is a random walk, this is not accurate. Rather, the underlying behavior of consumers makes both consumption and wealth evolve as random walks.

All the theoretical results presented in this section rest on the assumption that consumers face a known, constant, real interest rate. If the real interest rate varies over time in a way that is known for certain in advance the results will remain true with minor amendments—mainly, λ_t will vary over time on this account. The importance of known variations in interest rates depends on the elasticity of substitution between the present and future. If that elasticity is low, the influence will be unimportant. On the other hand, if the real interest rate applicable between periods t and $t + 1$ is uncertain at the time the consumption decision in period t is made, then the theoretical results no longer apply. However, there seems no strong reason for this to bias the results of the statistical tests in one direction or another.

4.2   Tests to Distinguish the Life-Cycle–Permanent Income Theory from Alternative Theories

The tests of the stochastic of the life-cycle–permanent income hypothesis carried out in this paper all have the form of estimating a conditional expectation, $E(c_t | c_{t-1}, x_{t-1})$, where x_{t-1} is a vector of data known in period $t - 1$, and then testing the hypothesis that the conditional expectation is actually not a function of x_{t-1}.[4] In all cases, the conditional expectation is made linear in x_{t-1}, so the tests are the usual F-tests for the exclusion of a group of variables from a regression. Again, regression is the appropriate statistical technique for estimating the conditional expectation, and no claim is made that the true structural relation between consumption and its determinants is revealed by this approach.

What departures from the life-cycle–permanent income hypothesis will this kind of test detect? There are two principal lines of thought about consumption that contradict the hypothesis. One holds that consumers are unable to smooth consumption over transitory fluctuations in income because of liquidity constraints and other practical considerations. Consumption is therefore too sensitive to current income to conform to the life-cycle–permanent income principle. The second holds that a reasonable measure of permanent income is a distributed lag of past actual income, so the consumption function should relate actual consumption to such a distributed lag. A general consumption function embodying both ideas might let consumption respond with a fairly large coefficient to contemporaneous income and then have a distributed lag over past income. Such consumption functions are in widespread use and fit the data extremely well. But their estimation involves the very substantial issue that income and consumption are jointly determined. Estimation by least squares provides no evidence whether the observed behavior is consistent with the life-cycle–permanent income hypothesis or not. Simultaneous estimation could provide evidence, but it would rest on crucial assumptions of exogeneity. Regressions of consumption on lagged consumption and lagged income *can* provide evidence without assumptions of exogeneity, as this section will show.

Consider first the issue of excessive sensitivity of consumption to transityory fluctuations in income, which has been emphasized by Tobin and Dolde (1971) and Mishkin (1976). The simplest alternative hypothesis supposes that a fraction of the population simply consumes all its disposable income, instead of obeying the life-cycle–permanent income consumption function. Suppose this fraction earns a proportion μ of total income, and let $c_t' = \mu y_t$ be their consumption. The other part of consumption, say c_t'', follows the rule set out earlier: $c_t'' = \lambda c_{t-1}'' + \varepsilon_t$. The conditional expectation of total consumption, c_t, given its own lagged value, and, say, two lagged values of income, is $E(c_t | c_{t-1}, y_{t-1}, y_{t-2}) = E(c_t' | c_{t-1}, y_{t-1}, y_{t-2}) + E(c_t'' | c_{t-1}, y_{y-1}, y_{t-2}) = \mu E(y_t | c_{t-1}, y_{y-1}, y_{t-2}) + \lambda(c_{t-1} - \mu y_{y-1})$. Suppose that disposable income obeys univariate autoregressive process of second order, so $E(y_t | c_{t-1}, y_{y-1}, y_{t-2}) = \rho_1 y_{t-1} + \rho_2 y_{t-2}$. Then $E(c_t | c_{t-1}, y_{y-1}, y_{t-2}) = \lambda c_{t-1} + \mu(\rho_1 - \lambda) y_{t-1} + \mu \rho_2 y_{t-2}$. The life-cycle–permanent income hypothesis will be rejected unless $\rho_1 = \lambda$ and $\rho_2 = 0$, that is, unless disposable income and consumption obey exactly the same stochastic process. If they do, permanent income and observed income are the same thing, and the liquidity-constrained fraction of the population is obeying the hypothesis anyway, so the hypothesis is confirmed. The proposed test involving regressing c_t on c_{t-1}, y_{y-1}, and y_{t-2} will reject the life-cycle–permanent income hypothesis in favor of the simple liquidity-constrained model whenever the latter is materially different from the former.

The distributed lag approximation to permanent income was first suggested by Friedman (1957, 1963) and has figured prominently in consumption functions ever since. Distributed lags are not necessarily incompatible with the life-cycle–permanent income hypothesis—if income obeys a stable stochastic process, there should be a structural relation between the innovation in income and consumption (Flavin 1977).[5] Still, the theory of the consumer presented earlier rules out any extra predictive value of a distributed lag of income (excluding contemporaneous income) in a regression that contains lagged consumption. If consumers use a nonoptimal distributed lag in forming their estimates of permanent income, then this central implication of the life-cycle–permanent income hypothesis is false. This proposition is easiest to establish for the simple Koyck or geometric distributed lag, $c_t = \alpha \sum_{i=0}^{\infty} \beta^i y_{t-i}$ or $c_t = \beta c_{t-1} + \alpha y_t$. Suppose, as before, that y_t obeys second-order autoregressive process, $E(y_t | c_{t-1}, y_{y-1}, y_{t-2}) =$

$\rho_1 y_{t-1} + \rho_2 y_{t-2}$. Then the conditional expectation is $E(c_t | c_{t-1}, y_{y-1}, y_{t-2}) = \beta c_{t-1} + \alpha \rho_1 y_{y-1} + \alpha \rho_2 y_{t-2}$. As long as income is serially correlated ($\rho_1 \neq 0$ or $\rho_2 \neq 0$), this conditional expectation will not depend solely on c_{t-1} and the pure life-cycle–permanent income hypothesis will be refuted. Discussion of the peculiarities of the case of uncorrelated income seems unnecessary, since income is in fact highly serially correlated. With this slight qualification, the proposed test procedure will always detect a Koyck lag if it is present and thus refute the life-cycle–permanent income hypothesis.

It is possible to show that the test also applies to the general distributed lag model used by Modigliani (1971) and others. If the lag in the underlying structural consumption function is nonoptimal, lagged income will have additional predictive power for current consumption beyond that of lagged consumption, so the life-cycle–permanent income hypothesis will be rejected. Data generated by consumers who use an optimal distributed lag of current and past income in making consumption decisions will not cause rejection. This shows the crucial distinction between structural models, which include contemporaneous income, and the test regressions of this paper, where the principle of the tests involves the inclusion of lagged variables alone.

This section has shown that simple tests of the predictive power of variables other than lagged consumption can detect departures from the pure life-cycle–permanent income hypothesis in the two directions that have been widely suggested in previous research on consumption. Both excessive sensitivity to current income because of liquidity constraints and nonoptimal distributed lag behavior will give additional predictive power to lagged income beyond that of lagged consumption in a regression for current consumption. The discussion of this section focused on the possible role of lagged income because that role is so closely related to alternative theories of consumption. Valid tests can be performed with any variable that is known in period $t - 1$ or earlier. The additional tests presented in the next section use extra lagged values of consumption and lagged values of common stock prices. Both variables have plausible justifications, but are less closely related to competing theories of consumption.

4.3   The Data and Results for the Basic Model

The most careful research on consumption has distinguished between the investment and consumption activities of consumers by removing investment in consumer durables and adding the imputed service flow of the stock of durables to consumption. For the purposes of this paper, however, it is more satisfactory simply to examine consumption of nondurables and services. All the theoretical foundations of the aggregate consumption function apply to individual categories of consumption as well. Dropping durables altogether avoids the suspicion that the findings are an artifact of the procedure for imputing a service flow to the stock of durables. The data on consumption used throughout the study, then, can be defined exactly as consumption of nondurables and services in 1972 dollars from the U.S. National Income and Product Accounts divided by the population. All data are quarterly.

Table 4.1 presents the results of fitting the basic regression relation between current and lagged marginal utility predicted by the pure life cycle–permanent income theory. Equations 4.1 and 4.2 are for the constant-elasticity utility function, with $\sigma = 0.2$ and 1.0, respectively. Equation 4.3 is for the quadratic utility function exactly, or for any utility function approximately, and is simply a regression of consumption on its own lagged value and a constant. All three equations show that the predictive value of lagged marginal utility for current marginal utility is extremely high; that is, the typical information that becomes available in each quarter, as measured by ε_t, has only a small impact on consumption or marginal utility. Of course, this is no more than a theoretical interpretation of the well-known fact that consumption is highly serially correlated. The close fit of the regressions in table 4.1 is not itself confirmation of the life-cycle–permanent income hypothesis, since the hypothesis makes no prediction about the variability of permanent income and the resultant variance of ε_t.

Table 4.1
Regression results for the basic model 1948–77 ($c_t^{-1/\sigma} = \gamma c_{t-1}^{-1/\sigma} + \varepsilon_t$)

Equation	σ	Constant	γ	SE	R^2	D-W statistic
4.0	0.2	...	0.983 (0.003)	0.000735	0.9964	2.06
4.2	1.0	...	0.996 (0.001)	0.00271	0.9985	1.83
4.3	-1.0	$-.014$	1.011 (0.003)	0.0146	0.9988	1.70

Note: The numbers in parentheses in these and subsequent regressions are standard errors.

The theory is compatible with any amount of unexplained variation in the regression.

There is no usable statistical criterion for choice among the three equations in table 4.1. The transformation of the dependent variable rules out the simple principle of least squares. Under the assumption of a normal distribution for ε_t, there is a likelihood function with an extra term, the Jacobian determinant, to take account of the transformation. However, for this sample, it proved to be an increasing function of σ for all values, so no maximum-likelihood estimator is available. This seems to reflect the operation of corollary 5—the ε_t's are small enough that any specification of marginal utility is essentially proportional to consumption itself, and the effective content of the life-cycle–permanent income theory is to make consumption itself evolve as a random walk with trend. From this point on, the paper will discuss only equation 4.13 and its extensions to other variables.

The principal stochastic implication of the life-cycle–permanent income hypothesis is that no other variables observed in quarter $t - 1$ or earlier can help predict the residuals from the regressions in table 4.1. Before formal statistical tests are used, it is useful to study the residuals themselves. The pattern of the residuals is extremely similar in the three regressions, but the residuals themselves are easiest to interpret for equation 1.3, where they have the units of consumption per capita in 1972 dollars. These residuals appear in table 4.2.

The standard error of the residuals in 14.6, so roughly six of the observations should exceed 29.2 in magnitude. There are in fact six. Three are drops in consumption, and of these, one coincides with the standard dating of recessions: 1974:4. Five milder recessions contribute drops of less than two standard deviations: 1949:3, 1953:4, 1958:1, 1960:3, and 1970:4. The other major decline in consumption is associated with the Korean War, in 1950:4. Most of the drops in consumption occurred quickly, in one or two quarters. The only important exception was in the period from 1973:4 to 1975:1, when six straight quarters of consecutive decline took place. On the expansionary side, there is little consistent evidence of any systematic tendency for consumption to recover in a regular pattern after a setback. The largest single increase occurred in 1965:4. This, together with three successive increases in 1964, accounts for all of the increase in consumption relative to trend associated with the prolonged boom of the mid- and late 1960s.

Table 4.2
Residuals from regression of consumption on lagged consumption, 1948–77 ($)

1948:		1956:		1964:		1972:	
1....	0.5	1....	2.8	1....	17.8	1....	20.0
2....	8.0	2....	−10.1	2....	20.0	2....	32.7
3....	−15.5	3....	−6.1	3....	14.6	3....	8.4
4....	3.5	4....	1.2	4....	−4.4	4....	21.1
1949:		1957:		1965:		1973:	
1....	−8.6	1....	−10.8	1....	5.8	1....	8.0
2....	−8.5	2....	−6.1	2....	5.2	2....	−15.6
3....	−27.2	3....	2.4	3....	10.2	3....	3.0
4....	−0.1	4....	−13.6	4....	38.7	4....	−32.8
1950:		1958:		1966:		1974:	
1....	5.6	1....	−29.1	1....	−1.3	1....	−27.3
2....	23.8	2....	8.3	2....	3.7	2....	−23.4
3....	15.5	3....	14.3	3....	−1.9	3....	−16.6
4....	−31.0	4....	−1.9	4....	−12.4	4....	−42.8
1951:		1959:		1967:		1975:	
1....	16.0	1....	15.1	1....	10.2	1....	−5.8
2....	−24.8	2....	3.8	2....	2.0	2....	25.6
3....	9.0	3....	−2.7	3....	−2.8	3....	−21.3
4....	−6.1	4....	1.1	4....	−7.5	4....	0.9
1952:		1960:		1968:		1976:	
1....	−15.1	1....	−5.6	1....	15.6	1....	24.4
2....	18.0	2....	8.8	2....	7.9	2....	8.3
3....	10.0	3....	−24.3	3....	22.2	3....	2.3
4....	8.6	4....	−10.1	4....	−8.1	4....	30.4
1953:		1961:		1969:		1977:	
1....	−1.6	1....	1.8	1....	0.8	1....	−1.8
2....	−1.0	2....	10.1	2....	−5.3		
3....	−22.1	3....	−16.9	3....	−2.4		
4....	−27.0	4....	15.8	4....	0.3		
1954:		1962:		1970:			
1....	−0.1	1....	−1.7	1....	4.0		
2....	−2.4	2....	3.4	2....	−12.3		
3....	11.9	3....	−0.8	3....	−0.3		
4....	7.4	4....	0.6	4....	−21.5		
1955:		1963:		1971:			
1....	6.1	1....	−8.4	1....	1.5		
2....	7.0	2....	−1.3	2....	−2.4		
3....	−0.8	3....	11.7	3....	−14.6		
4....	22.3	4....	−6.3	4....	−6.6		

The data contain no obvious refutation of the unpredictability of the residuals from the basic model, but, just as a study of stock prices will never convince the "chartist" that it is futile to try to predict their future, the confirmed believer in regular fluctuations in consumption will not be swayed by the data alone. More powerful methods for summarizing the data are required.

4.4 Can Consumption Be Predicted from Its Own Past Values?

The simplest testable implication of the pure life-cycle–permanent income hypothesis is that only the first lagged value of consumption helps predict current consumption. This implication would be refuted if consumption had a definite cyclical pattern described by a difference equation of second or higher order.[6] Intelligent consumers ought to be able to offset any such cyclical pattern and restore the noncyclical optimal behavior of consumption predicted by the hypothesis. The following regression tests this implication by adding additional lagged values of consumption to equation 4.3.

$$c_t = 8.2 + 1.130c_{t-1} - 0.040c_{t-2} + 0.030c_{t-3} - 0.113c_{t-4};$$
$$\quad (8.3) \quad (0.92) \qquad (0.142) \qquad (0.142) \qquad (0.093)$$

$$R^2 = 0.9988, \quad s = 14.5; \quad \text{D-W} = 1.96.$$

The contribution of the extra lagged values is to increase the accuracy of the forecast of current consumption by about 10 cents per person per year. The F-statistic for the hypothesis that the coefficients of c_{t-2}, c_{t-3} and c_{t-4} are all zero is 1.7, well under the critical point of the F-distribution of 2.7 at the 5% level. Only very weak evidence against the pure life cycle–permanent income hypothesis appears in this regression. In particular, there are no definite signs that consumption obeys a second-order difference equation capable of generating stochastic cycles. In this respect, consumption differs sharply from other aggregate economic measures, which do typically obey second-order autoregressions.

4.5 Can Consumption Be Predicted from Disposable Income?

If lagged income has substantial predictive power beyond that of lagged consumption, then the life cycle–permanent income hypothesis is refuted.

As discussed in section 4.2, this evidence would support the alternative views that consumers are excessively sensitive to current income, or, more generally, that they use an ad hoc, nonoptimal distributed of past income in making consumption decisions.

Table 4.3 presents a variety of regressions testing the predictive power of real disposable income per capita, measured as current dollar disposable income from the national accounts divided by implicit deflator for consumption of nondurables and services and divided by population. Equation 4.4 shows that a single lagged level of disposable income has essentially no predictive value at all. The coefficient of y_{t-1} is slightly negative, but this is easily explained by sampling variation alone. The F-statistic for the exclusion of all but the constant and c_{t-1} is 0.1, far below the critical F of 3.9. Equation 4.5 tries a year-long distributed lag estimated without constraint. The first lagged value of disposable income has a slight positive coefficient, but this is more than outweighed by the three negative coefficients for the longer lags. The long-run "marginal propensity to consume," measured by the sum of the coefficients, is actually negative, though again this could easily result from sampling variation. The F-statistic for the joint predictive value of all four lagged income variables is 2.0, somewhat less than the critical value of 2.4 at the 5% level. Note that the pure life-cycle–permanent income hypothesis would be rejected if the size of the test were 10% or higher.

Equation 4.6 fits a 12-quarter Almon lag to see if a long distributed lag can compete with lagged consumption as a predictor for current consumption. Again, the sum of the lag coefficients is slightly negative, now almost significantly so. The F-statistic for the hypothesis of no contribution from the complete distributed lag on income is again close to the critical value.

The sample evidence of the relation between consumption and lagged income seems to say the following: There is a statistically marginal and numerically small relation between consumption and very recent levels of disposable income. The sum of the lag coefficients is slightly negative. Further, there is no evidence at all supporting the view that a long distributed lag covering several years helps to predict consumption. This evidence casts just a little doubt on the life cycle–permanent income hypothesis in its purest form but is not at all destructive to a somewhat more flexible interpretation of the hypothesis, to be discussed shortly.

Table 4.3
Equations relating consumption to lagged consumption and past levels of real disposable income

Equation number	Equation	R^2	s	D-W	F	F*
4.4...........	$c_t = -16 + 1.024c_{t-1} - 0.010y_{t-1}$ (11) (0.044) (0.032)	0.9988	14.7	1.71	0.1	3.9
4.5...........	$c_t = -23 + 1.076c_{t-1} + 0.049y_{t-1} - 0.051y_{t-2}$ (11) (0.047) (0.043) (0.052) $-0.023y_{t-3} - 0.024y_{t-4}$ (0.051) (0.037)	0.9989	14.4	2.02	2.0	2.4
4.6...........	$c_t = -25 + 1.113c_{t-1} + \sum_{i=1}^{12} \beta_i y_{t-1} + \Sigma\beta_i = 0.077$ (11) (0.054) (0.040)	0.9988	14.6	1.92	2.0	2.7

4.6   Wealth and Consumption

Of the many alternative variables that might be included on the right-hand side of a regression to test the pure life-cycle–permanent income hypothesis, some measure of wealth is one of the leading candidates. Theory and prevailing practice agree that contemporaneous wealth has a strong influence on consumption, so lagged wealth is a logical variable to test. Again, the hypothesis implies that wealth measured in earlier quarters should have no predictive value with respect to this quarter's consumption. All information contained in lagged wealth should be summarized in lagged consumption.

Reliable quarterly data on property values are not available for most categories of property. For one major category, however, essentially perfect data are available at any frequency, namely, the market value of corporate stock. Tests of the random-walk hypothesis do not require a comprehensive wealth variable, so a test based on stock prices is appropriate, even though the resulting equation does not describe the structural relation between wealth and consumption. The tests reported here are based on Standard and Poor's comprehensive index of the prices of stocks deflated by the implicit deflator for nondurables and services and divided by population. This variable will be called s. It makes a statistically unambiguous contribution to prediction of current consumption:

$$c = -22 + 1.012c_{t-1} + 0.223s_{t-1} - 0.258s_{t-2} + 0.167s_{t-3} - 0.120s_{t-4}$$
$$(8) \quad (0.004) \quad (0.051) \quad (0.083) \quad (0.083) \quad (0.051)$$

$$R^2 = 0.9990; \quad SE = 1.4; \quad D\text{-}W = 2.05.$$

The F-statistic for the hypothesis that the coefficients of the lagged stock prices are all zero is 6.5, well above the critical value of 2.4 at the 5% level. Further, each coefficient considered separately is clearly different from zero according to the usual t-test. However, the improvement in the predictive power of the regression, while statistically significant, is not numerically large. The standard error of the regression is about 20 cents per person per year smaller in this equation compared with the basic model of equation 4.3 ($14.40 against $14.60). Most of the predictive value of the stock price comes from the *change* in the price in the immediately preceding quarter. A smaller contribution is made by the change in the price three quarters earlier. Use of the Almon lag technique for both levels and differences in the stock price failed to turn up any evidence of a longer distributed lag.

4.7   Implications of the Empirical Evidence

The pure life-cycle–permanent income hypothesis—that c_t cannot be predicted by any variable dated $t - 1$ or earlier other than c_{t-1}—is rejected by the data. The stock market is valuable in predicting consumption one quarter in the future. Most of the predictive power comes from Δs_{t-1}. But the data seem entirely compatible with a modification of the hypothesis that leaves its central content unchanged. Suppose that consumption does depend on permanent income, and the marginal utility indeed does evolve as a random walk with trend, but that some part of consumption takes time to adjust to a change in permanent income. Then any variable that is correlated with permanent income in $t - 1$ will help in predicting the change in consumption in period t, since part of that change is the lagged response to the previous change in permanent income. Both the finding that consumption is only weakly associated with its own past values and that immediate past values of changes in stock prices have a modest predictive value are compatible with this modification of the life cycle–permanent income hypothesis.

Whatever problems remain in the consumption function, there seems little reason to doubt the life-cycle–permanent income hypothesis. Within a framework in which permanent income is treated as an unobserved variable the data seem fully compatible with the hypothesis, provided a short lag between permanent income and consumption is recognized. Of course, acceptance of the hypothesis does not yield a complete consumption function, since no equation for permanent income has been developed. The evidence against the ad hoc distributed-lag model relating permanent income to actual income seems fairly strong. The task of further research is to create a more satisfactory model for permanent income, one that recognizes that consumers appraise their economic well-being in an intelligent way that involves looking into the future.

It is important not to treat any of the equations of this paper as structural relations between consumption and the variables that are used to predict it. For example, table 4.3 should not be read as implying that income has a negative effect on consumption. The effect of a particular change in income depends on the change in permanent income it induces, and this can range anywhere from no effect to a dollar-for-dollar effect, depending on the way that consumers evaluate the change. In any case, the regressions understate the true structural relation between the change in income and

the change in consumption because they omit the contemporaneous part
of the relation.

4.8 Implications for Forecasting and Policy Analysis

Under the pure life-cycle–permanent income hypothesis, a forecast of
future consumption obtained by extrapolating today's level by the historical trend is impossible to improve. The results of this paper have the strong
implication that beyond the next few quarters consumption should be
treated as an exogenous variable. There is no point in forecasting future
income and then relating it to income, since any information available
today about future income is already incorporated in today's permanent
income. Forecasts of consumption next quarter can be improved slightly
with current stock prices, but no further improvement can be achieved in
this way in later quarters.

With respect to the analysis of stabilization policy, the findings of this
paper go no further than supporting the view that policy affects consumption only as much as it affects permanent income. In the analysis of policies
that are known to leave permanent income unchanged, consumption may
be treated as exogenous. Further, only *new* information about taxes and
other policy instruments can affect permanent income. Beyond these general propositions, the policy analyst must answer the difficult question of
the effect of a given policy on permanent income in order to predict its effect
on consumption. Regression of consumption on current and past values of
income are no value whatever in answering this question.

Appendix

THEOREM.   If a consumer maximizes $E_t \sum_{t=0}^{T} (1 + \delta)^{-t} u(c_t)$, subject to $\sum_{t=0}^{T}$
$(1 + r)^{-t}(c_t - w_t) = A_0$, sequentially determining c_t at each t, then $E_t u'(c_{t+1})$
$= [(1 + \delta)/(1 + r)] \times u'(c_t)$.

Proof.   At time t, the consumer chooses c_t so as to maximize $(1 + \delta)^{-t} u(c_t)$
$+ E_t \sum_{\tau=t+1}^{T} (1 + \delta)^{-t} u(c_\tau)$ subject to $\sum_{\tau=t}^{T} (1 + r)^{(\tau-t)}(c_\tau - w_\tau) = A_t$. The optimal sequential strategy has the form $c_\tau = g_\tau(w_\tau, w_{\tau-1}, \ldots, w_0, A_0)$. Consider
a variation from this strategy: $c_t = g_t(w_t, \ldots) + x$: $c_{t+1} = g_{t+1}(w_{t+1}, w_t, \ldots) -$
$(1 + r)x$.

Note that the new consumption strategy also satisfies the budget constraint. Now consider $\max_x\{(1 + \delta)^{-t}u(g_t + x) + E_t[(1 + \delta)^{-t-1}u(g_{t+1} - (1 + r)x) + \sum_{\tau=t+2}^{T} (1 + \delta)^{-\tau}u(g_\tau)]\}$.

The first-order condition is $(1 + \delta)^{-t}u'(g_t + x) - E_t(1 + \delta)^{-t-1}(1 + r) u'(g_{t+1} - (1 + r)x) = 0$ as asserted.

Proof of Corollary 5. Recall that $u'(c_{t+1}) = [(1 + \delta)/(1 + r)]u'(c_t) + \varepsilon_{t+1}$ and $\lambda_t = [(1 + \delta)/(1 + r)]^{u'(c_t)/[c_t u''(c_t)]}$. Expand the implicit equation for c_{t+1} in a Taylor series at the point $\lambda_t = 1 (r = \delta)$ and $\varepsilon_{t+1} = 0: c_{t+1} = c_t + (\lambda_t - 1) (\partial c_{t+1}/\partial \lambda_t) + \varepsilon_{t+1}(\partial c_{t+1}/\partial \varepsilon_{t+1}) +$ higher-order terms. At the point $\lambda_t = 1$ and $\varepsilon_{t+1} = 0$, c_{t+1} equals c_t, and it is not hard to show that $\partial c_{t+1}/\partial \lambda_t = c_t$ and $\partial c_{t+1}/\partial \varepsilon_{t+1} = 1/u''(c_t)$. Thus $c_{t+1} = c_t + (\lambda_t - 1)c_t + \varepsilon_{t+1}/u''(c_t) = \lambda_t c_t + \varepsilon_{t+1}/u''(c_t)$, as asserted.

Notes

This research was supported by the National Science Foundation. I am grateful to Marjorie Flavin for assistance and to numerous colleagues for helpful suggestions.

1. Examples are Darby (1972) and Blinder (1977).

2. An illuminating analysis of the behavior of consumption when income is stationary appears in Yaari (1976). Further aspects are discussed by Bewley (1976).

3. Granger and Newbold (1976) present much stronger results for a similar problem but assume a normal distribution for the disturbance.

4. The nature of the hypothesis being tested and the statistical tests themselves are essentially the same as in the large body of research on efficient capital markets (see Fama 1970). Sims (1978) treats the statistical problem of the asymptotic distribution of the regression coefficients of x_{t-1} in this kind of regression, with the conclusion that the standard formulas are correct.

5. Lucas (1976) argues convincingly that the stochastic process for income will shift if policy rules change.

6. Fama (1970) calls the similar test for asset prices a "weak form" test.

References

Bewley, Truman. 1976. "The Permanent Income Hypothesis: A Theoretical Formulation." Mimeographed. Cambridge, Mass.: Harvard Univ., Dept. Econ., September.

Blinder, Alan. 1977. "Temporary Taxes and Consumer Spending." Mimeographed. Jerusalem: Inst. Advanced Studies, April.

Darby, Michael R. 1972. "The Allocation of Transitory Income among Consumers' Assets." *A.E.R.* 62 (December): 928–41.

Fama, Eugene F. 1970. "Efficient Capital Markets: A Review of Theory and Empirical Work." *J. Finance* 25 (May): 383–417.

Flavin, Marjorie. 1977. "The Adjustment of Consumption to Changing Expectations about Future Income." Unpublished paper, Massacusetts Inst. Tech., February.

Friedman, Milton. 1957. *A Theory of the Consumption Function.* Princeton, N.J.: Princeton Univ. Press.

Friedman, Milton. 1963. "Windfalls, the 'Horizon,' and Related Concepts in the Permanent-Income Hypothesis." In *Measurement in Economics: Studies in Mathematical Economics and Econometrics in Memory of Yehuda Grunfeld,* edited by Carl Christ et al. Stanford, Calf.: Stanford Univ. Press.

Friedman, Milton, and Becker, Gary S. 1957. "A Statistical Illusion in Judging Keynesian Models." *J.P.E.* 65, no. 1 (February): 64–75.

Granger, C. W. J., and Newbold, P. 1976 "Forecasting Transformed Series." *J. Royal Statis. Soc.* ser. B, 38, no. 2: 189–203.

Haavelmo, Trygve. 1943. "The Statistical Implications of a System of Simultaneous Equations." *Econometrica* 11 (January): 1–12.

Lucas, Robert E., Jr. 1976. "Econometric Policy Evaluation: A Critique." In *The Phillips Curve and Labor Markets,* edited by Karl Brunner and Allan H. Meltzer. Carnegie-Rochester Conference Series on Public Policy. Amsterdam: North-Holland; New York: American Elsevier.

Mishkin, Frederic. 1976. "Illiquidity, Consumer Durable Expenditure, and Monetary Policy." *A.E.R.* 66 (September): 642–54.

Modigliani, Franco. 1971. "Monetary Policy and Consumption." In *Consumer Spending and Monetary Policy: The Linkages.* Conference Series No. 5. Boston: Federal Reserve Bank of Boston.

Sims, Christopher A. 1978. "Least Squares Estimation of Autoregressions with Some Unit Roots." Discussion Paper no. 78–95, Univ. Minnesota, Center Econ. Res., March.

Tobin, James, and Dolde, Walter. 1971. "Wealth, Liquidity, and Consumption." In *Consumer Spending and Monetary Policy: The Linkages.* Conference Series No. 5. Boston: Federal Reserve Bank of Boston.

Yaari, Menahem E. 1976. "A Law of Large Numbers in the Theory of Consumer's Choice under Uncertainty." *J. Econ. Theory* 12 (April): 202–17.

5 The Sensitivity of Consumption to Transitory Income: Estimates from Panel Data on Households

(with Frederic S. Mishkin)

The stochastic relationship of consumption to income has long been recognized as a critical issue to macropolicy analysis. One traditional view of consumers sees them as largely passive agents in the detemination of aggregate demand. Changes in real incomes are translated reasonably quickly and fully into changes in consumption. In this view, income changes brought about by tax changes are a powerful tool for countercyclical stabilization policy, as Okun (1971) and Tobin and Dolde (1971) have argued. In contrast, the life-cycle–permanent income hypothesis of consumption embodies the opposite view that consumers maximize utility over a long-term horizon. Rather than responding passively to every change in income, consumers will alter their consumption by smaller amounts if they perceive the income change as temporary rather than permanent. Eisner (1969) has argued along this line. With the refinement of rational expectations, the life-cycle–permanent income theory (as in Muth (1960), Lucas (1976), and Hall (1978)) casts serious doubt on the usefulness of income variations as a stabilization tool. Consumers cannot be relied on to react vigorously when a policy-induced income change occurs. Predicting the impact of an income change on consumption requires knowledge of consumers' perceptions of its permanence.

This paper tries to shed some light on the stochastic relation between income and consumption (specifically, consumption of food) within a panel of about 2000 households who reported both variables over a 7-year span. Our major findings are as follows:

1. Consumption responds much more strongly to permanent than to transitory movements of income.

2. The response to transitory income is nonetheless vigorous; it makes sense within the model only if interest rates are at least 20%.

3. A simple test, independent of our model of consumption, rejects the pure life-cycle–permanent income hypothesis.

4. The observed covariation of income and consumption is compatible with pure life-cycle–permanent income behavior for 80% of consumption and simple proportionality of consumption and income for the remaining 20%.

Reprinted with permission from "The Sensitivity of Consumption to Transitory Income: Estimates from Panel Data on Households" (with Frederic Mishkin), *Econometrica*, vol. 50, no. 2, March 1982, pp. 461–481.

These conclusions are derived from evidence about the joint movements of income and consumption. Needless to say, consumption and income frequently rise or fall together in the same year for a particular family. Our model explains the bulk of this correlation as the immediate response of consumption to changes in permanent income. Most of the rest is attributed to departures from life-cycle–permanent income behavior for a small part of consumption. We hypothesize that about a fifth of all consumption is just set to a fraction of current income instead of following the more complicated optimal rule.

The nature of our data precludes any examination of intertemporal substitution effects in consumption. Thus our results do not answer the question of possible effects of temporary tax policies via substitution rather than income effects. Using time-series data, Hall (1980) finds that intertemporal substitution is apparently weak for total consumption of nondurable goods.

5.1   Stochastic Theory of Consumer Behavior

An important paper by John Muth (1960) on the permanent income hypothesis showed that the marginal propensities to consume out of current and lagged income depend on the stochastic properties of income. An income process with a large transitory component implies a small propensity to consume out of current income. At the other extreme, when most changes in income are permanent—that is, when income is almost a random walk—the propensity to consume out of current income should differ only slightly from the propensity to consume out of permanent income. This point was overlooked in empirical work on consumption long after the publication of Muth's article; Mayer's (1972b) survey does not mention any studies that consider the issue, for example. In recent work using data on individual consumers (Mayer 1972a), estimates of large propensities to consume out of current income are interpreted as evidence against the permanent income hypothesis without any discussion of the stochastic process of income. The evidence is actually ambiguous because the permanent income hypothesis together with plausible income processes could well imply exactly the degree of sensitivity found.

Recent work by Hall (1978) deals with some of these problems by deriving a theory of the stochastic process of consumption from the life-cycle–permanent income hypothesis. Empirical tests then find that one of the important implications of the hypothesis is largely supported by aggregate time series data.[1] A recent paper by Flavin (1981) examines aggregate data in a framework similar to the one used here, again with generally favorable results. However, aggregate evidence is not really powerful enough to settle the important questions about the behavior of consumers.

These considerations have led to the research reported here based on data for individual households. We bring a rather specific question to this research: Are consumers more sensitive to current fluctuations in income than they would be if they followed the dictates of the life-cycle–permanent income model? We approach the question in the following way: First, we propose a stochastic model of household income. Then, we hypothesize that households choose current consumption so as to maximize expected intertemporal utility, as suggested by the life-cycle–permanent income view of consumption. In so doing, they arrive at an estimate of permanent income, based on the information available about the various stochastic components of actual income. Note that permanent income is not one of the components we hypothesize for actual income. Rather, permanent income is an intermediate step in the process by which families determine consumption. In this respect, we expand on earlier microeconomic research on the permanent income hypothesis. The final step makes observed consumption equal to a fraction of permanent income plus a transitory component which can be interpreted as measurement error, inventory accumulation, and the like.

The empirical analysis in this paper focuses on the theoretical implication that consumers should increase consumption by the annuity value of the increase in wealth brought about by a transitory increase in income. We test this implication by estimating the model using panel data on the income and consumption levels of individuals over several years. However, the response of consumption to the transitory component of income is estimated as a free parameter rather than constraining it to equal the expression for the annuity value. We then can evaluate whether consumption is excessively responsive to current income.

The starting point for our work is the life-cycle–permanent income theory of consumption. According to the theory, consumers form estimates of lifetime resources and then adopt plans for spreading those resources over the remining years of their lives. With explicit consideration of uncertainty (Yaari 1976, Bewley 1976, and Hall 1978), this principle becomes: consumers form estimates of the probability distributions of lifetime resources and adopt sequential policies for spreading the resources. We will consider the hypothesis of rational expectations which asserts that consumers use all available information in estimating the probability distributions of future resources. This hypothesis is more of a sharpening and clarification of assumptions already implicit in the life-cycle–permanent income theory rather than a logically independent assumption.

Here we consider the case of a household whose real income is the sum of three components: (1) a deterministic component, $\bar{y}_t$, which rises with age until just before retirement and then falls rapidly; (2) a stochastic component, y_t^L, which fluctuates as lifetime prospects change; because this lifetime component embodies information about essentially permanent family characteristics, a natural specification is a random walk; (3) a stationary stochastic component y_t^S, which fluctuates according to transitory influences and is described by a moving average time-series process.

We use the following stochastic model of household income:

$$y_t = \bar{y}_t + y_t^L + y_t^S, \tag{1}$$

$$y_t^L = y_{t-1}^L + \varepsilon_t, \tag{2}$$

$$y_t^S = \sum_{m=0}^{\infty} \phi_m \eta_{t-m} \qquad (\phi_0 \text{ is normalized to equal 1}), \tag{3}$$

where ε_t and η_t are random innovations that are completely unpredictable from past information. A key feature of our model is the hypothesis that families separately know the two stochastic components of income, ε_t and η_t.

With a quadratic utility function, $u(\tilde{c}_t) = -\frac{1}{2}(c_t^* - \tilde{c}_t)^2$ (where c_t^* is the bliss level of consumption and $\tilde{c}_t$ is consumption), the household's intertemporal decision problem is to maximize

$$E_t \left[-\frac{1}{2} \sum_{\tau=0}^{T-t} (1 + \delta)^{-\tau} (c_{t+\tau}^* - \tilde{c}_{t+\tau})^2 \right] \tag{4}$$

subject to the budget constraint[2]

$$\sum_{\tau=0}^{T-t} (1 + r)^{-\tau} (y_{t+\tau} - \tilde{c}_{t+\tau}) + \tilde{A}_t = 0, \tag{5}$$

where E_t is mathematical expectation conditional on all information available at time t; δ is the subjective time preference; r is real rate of interest, which is assumed to be constant over time; T is length of economic life; $\tilde{c}_t$ consumption; c_t^* is bliss level of consumption; $\tilde{A}_t$ is nonhuman wealth (assets).

The first-order conditions for this problem are

$$\frac{E_t[(1 + \delta)^{-\tau}(c_{t+\tau}^* - \tilde{c}_{t+\tau})]}{c_t^* - \tilde{c}_t} = (1 + r)^{-\tau} \qquad \text{for } \tau = 1, \ldots, T - t. \tag{6}$$

For a derivation, see Hall (1978). This equation states the intuitively plausible result that the marginal rate of substitution between current and future income equals the price ratio between current and future consumption.

In order to simplify the model used in estimation, we assume that the household's rate of time discount, δ, equals the real interest rate, r. Empirical evidence in Hall (1978) does not call for rejection of this assumption, and it seems reasonable to make use of it in this paper's analysis. The first-order conditions now imply

$$E_t\tilde{c}_{t+\tau} = c_{t+\tau}^* + \tilde{c}_t - c_t^*. \tag{7}$$

Taking expectation conditional on information available at time t of the budget constraint and using (7) to substitute for $E_t\tilde{c}_{t+\tau}$, we have

$$\sum_{\tau=0}^{T-t} (1 + r)^{-\tau}[E_t y_{t+\tau} - c_{t+\tau}^* - \tilde{c}_t + c_t^*] + \tilde{A}_t = 0. \tag{8}$$

Defining human wealth at time t as $\tilde{H}_t$,

$$\tilde{H}_t \equiv \sum_{\tau=0}^{T-t} (1 + r)^{-\tau} E_t y_{t+\tau}, \tag{9}$$

and

$$\gamma_t \equiv \frac{1}{\sum_{\tau=0}^{T-t}(1 + r)^{-\tau}}, \tag{10}$$

$$\bar{V}_t \equiv \sum_{\tau=0}^{T-t} (1 + r)^{-\tau} c_{t+\tau}^*, \tag{11}$$

we can rewrite (8) as

$$\tilde{c}_t = c_t^* + \gamma_t(\tilde{H}_t + \tilde{A}_t - \bar{V}_t). \tag{12}$$

This consumption function tells us that an increase of one unit of either human or nonhuman wealth will result in an increase of consumption of

γ_t; γ_t is easily recognizable as the annuity value of one unit of wealth, that is, the stream of equal payments over the remainder of the lifetime that can be financed by a unit of wealth. For infinite horizons and small r it approximately equals the real interest rate, r. Thus this consumption function is identical to the life-cycle–permanent income consumption functions of Friedman (1957) and Ando and Modigliani (1963).

Further algebraic manipulation of the consumption function above is required to derive a model that can be estimated from the panel data used in this study. The deterministic paths of human and nonhuman wealth, denoted by $\bar{H}_t$ and $\bar{A}_t$, respectively, are defined as the paths of these variables that occur in the absence of surprises (innovations) in y^L and y^S (specifically, $\bar{H}_t \equiv \sum_{\tau=0}^{T-t}(1 + r)^{-\tau}\bar{y}_{t+\tau}$). The deterministic path of consumption, $\bar{c}_t$, is

$$\bar{c}_t = c_t^* + \gamma_t[\bar{H}_t + \bar{A}_t - \bar{V}_t]. \tag{13}$$

We subtract (13) from (12) and define c_t and A_t as deviations from the deterministic paths of consumption and assets—$c_t = \tilde{c}_t - \bar{c}_t$ and $A_t = \tilde{A}_t - \bar{A}_t$—to obtain

$$c_t = \gamma_t[H_t + A_t]. \tag{14}$$

The evolution of assets around their deterministic path is governed by

$$A_t = (1 + r)(A_{t-1} + y_{t-1}^L + y_{t-1}^S - c_{t-1}). \tag{15}$$

Since the real return to assets, r, is assumed to be constant, A_t is completely known at $t - 1$. The deviation of human wealth around its deterministic path can be written as

$$H_t = \sum_{\tau=0}^{T-t} (1 + r)^{-\tau}\left(y_t^L + \sum_{m=0}^{\infty} \varphi_{\tau+m}\eta_{t-m}\right) \tag{16}$$

$$= \frac{1}{\gamma_t}y_t^L + \sum_{m=0}^{\infty}\left(\sum_{\tau=0}^{T-t}(1 + r)^{-\tau}\varphi_{\tau+m}\right)\eta_{t-m}$$

$$= \frac{1}{\gamma_t}\varepsilon_t + \frac{1}{\gamma_t}y_{t-1}^L + \left(\sum_{\tau=0}^{T-t}(1 + r)^{-\tau}\varphi_\tau\right)\eta_t$$

$$+ \sum_{m=0}^{\infty}\left(\sum_{\tau=0}^{T-t}(1 + r)^{-\tau}\varphi_{\tau+m}\right)\eta_{t-m}.$$

The model to be estimated could be derived through additional tedious algebra, but an easier route to this derivation makes use of a proposition demonstrated by Hall (1978). Consumers with rational expectations who maximize the expected value of an intertemporally separable utility function of the type outlined here will display the following condition: No information available to this consumer at $t - 1$ beyond the value of consumption will help in predicting next period's marginal utility of consumption. In the case of the quadratic utility function used here and the assumption that $r = \delta$, this implies that c_t is a random walk and Δc_t will equal the unpredictable component of c_t. Because A_t, η_{t-m} for $m \geq 1$, and y_{t-1}^L are all known at time $t - 1$, the only unpredictable elements of the wealth term $H_t + A_t$ in (14) are those which involve the contemporaneous innovations ε_t and η_t. Hence, the change in consumption is γ_t times the innovation in H_t:

$$\Delta c_t = \varepsilon_t + \beta_t \eta_t, \tag{17}$$

where

$$\beta_t = \gamma_t \sum_{\tau=0}^{T-t} (1 + r)^{-\tau} \varphi_\tau;$$

this is the annuity value of the added wealth implied by a unit amount of unexpected transitory income. Equation 17 is a convenient form that can be estimated with the panel data available to us because it eliminates the need for information on household nonhuman assets.

Our empirical analysis focuses on the coefficient β_t, which is the marginal propensity to consume out of the transitory increase in income, y_t. The derived value of β_t above shows that it should equal the annuity value of the addition to wealth brought about by this transitory increase in income. Some illustrative values of β_t for the $MA(2)$ time-series model of y_t^S estimated in this paper where the moving average parameters are 0.2 at lag one and 0.1 at lag two are as follows:

		For real interest rate per year equal to			
		0.05	0.10	0.20	0.30
For remaining lifetime	20 years	0.095	0.105	0.170	0.232
	40 years	0.071	0.093	0.167	0.231

As these numbers indicate, rational consumption behavior is compatible with any degree of sensitivity to the surprise in the transitory income component (up to $\beta_t = 1$), provided a sufficiently high interest rate faces the consumer. No matter how much they discount the future, consumers should not simply make consumption proportional to current income; rather, the optimal strategy is to make the change in consumption respond only to the surprise in income and not to predictable movements of income. At very high interest rates, it is true that the information about future changes in income contained in today's surprise in income has negligible influence on wealth. However, it is still possible to take steps today that will insulate consumption from any foreseeable future changes in income. Exactly because the return to assets is high, a tiny amount saved from today's temporary increase in income can finance a complete offset of the subsequent decline in income later. In an economy with very high interest rates, consumers make small but lucrative and important asset transactions to achieve the optimal consumption path. Later in this chapter, we consider the behavior of consumers who are constrained against making any transactions in assets. They are prevented from achieving the optimal consumption path, and their actual consumption behaves in a way that is readily detectable in the data. There is a very substantial difference between optimal consumption in the face of very high interest rates and consumption constrained to equal current income.

As a final note on the interpretation of the theory, we emphasize that the lifetime component of income, y^L, is *not* the same thing as permanent income, although the propensity to consume out of y^L is the same as the propensity to consume out of permanent income. Permanent income includes the annuity values of transitory income and assets, as well as the lifetime component of income. Our research tries to make a clear distinction between the statistical decomposition of income into lifetime and transitory components, on the one hand, and the consumer's inference about permanent income, on the other hand.

5.2 Statistical Model and Estimation

The data for our investigation are obtained from the University of Michigan's Panel Study of Income Dynamics (PSID) which contains histories of earnings and spending for a large number of families over a span of several years. The PSID reports total annual family income net of estimated federal income taxes, which we then adjusted to take account of estimated FICA (social security) tax payments and changes in the overall cost of living (measured by the consumer price index). The most comprehensive and reliable consumption measure which can be obtained from the PSID is the sum of the annual expenditures on food used at home and the amount spent eating at restaurants. We deflated food expenditures with the food price component of the CPI. Data from the PSID for food consumption are available for the years 1969–1971 and 1973–1975 and for income for all years, 1969–1975. We included all families who reported income and food consumption in all years and whose responses to the food and income questions were deemed accurate by the interviewer.[3] We used data on six first differences of income and five first differences of consumption for 2309 families. One of the first differences of consumption spans two years; later in this section we describe how we accommodated this feature of the data.

In the PSID survey, information about food consumption is elicited by the question, How much do you spend on food in an average week? The question is asked sometime in the first half of the year; on the average the interview takes place at the end of March. We date the response in the previous year, as does the PSID. For a typical family interviewed in March 1971, for example, data on last year's income and usual food consumption are dated 1970 in our work. Because of the peculiar timing of the question about average food consumption, we found in necessary to extend the model described earlier in the paper in the following way. We assume that the new information about income which the family uses to decide on consumption dated in year t includes a fraction ϕ of the new information that will not be recorded by the survey until the following year. For the simple reason that the consumption question is asked partway into the following year, we might expect a value of ϕ near a quarter. However, a family might have access to additional information about income for the full year at the time that consumption is measured early in the year. For example, in some jobs annual compensation is known with near certainty at the beginning of the year. If this kind of advance information about income is commonplace, our estimate of ϕ should be correspondingly higher. We do not consider the possibility that consumers have information about income in years after $t + 1$, beyond what can be predicted from the history of income itself. Our low estimated value of ϕ tends to confirm our assumption on this point. Further details about the role of future information in the model and the estimation of ϕ appear in the next section.

In addition to the ambiguity about the timing of the question about food consumption, there is further ambiguity about the length of the period over which consumption is measured. Instead of asking about average consumption over an unstated period, it would be better for our purposes if it were about last year specifically or even about last week. We assume in the rest of this paper that the typical respondent averaged food consumption over a period much shorter than a year. In this case, the theory, which deals with consumption measured as an instantaneous flow, is a reasonable approximation for our data. Where consumption is measured as an average flow over an entire year, an explicit treatment of time aggregation is required.

The use of food consumption in place of total consumption obligates us to consider the form of the demand function for food, which differs in two respects from the demand function for total consumption. First, the price of food relative to the overall cost of living influences food consumption. Because all the families in the sample faced roughly the same change in relative prices, and our study relies primarily on the variability of individual family income, the relative price change presents few problems for our work. We posit equal relative price effects among families with similar characteristics and remove these effects before estimating the model. Details of this adjustment appear later in the paper.

The second consideration is the likelihood that the proportion of income spent on food declines as income rises—the usual view about the Engel curve for food. In the current research, we approximate the Engel curve by a straight line with a positive intercept. Though this does imply a declining expenditure fraction on food, it can be defended only as an approximation. The slope of the line will be called α; it is the marginal propensity to spend permanent income on food. The parameter β introduced in the previous section will be defined as the ratio of the marginal propensity to spend transitory income on food to the marginal propensity to spend lifetime income on food. Thus the units and the expected numerical values for β presented earlier will continue to apply.

Another extension of the basic model is necessary because food consumption is measured imperfectly. Any study of consumption at the level of individual households needs to include a stochastic element of measurement error and transitory consumption. We assume that measured consumption includes a transitory component, c_t^S, which obeys a second-order moving average process with parameters λ_1 and λ_2:

$$c_t^S = v_t + \lambda_1 v_{t-1} + \lambda_2 v_{t-2}. \tag{18}$$

We hypothesize that transitory consumption is uncorrelated with both components of income:

$$\text{corr}(v_t, \varepsilon_t) = \text{corr}(v_t, \eta_t) = 0. \tag{19}$$

With these various extensions, our model for the first difference of consumption becomes[4]

$$\Delta c_t = \alpha \varepsilon_t + \alpha \beta \eta_t + v_t - (1 - \lambda_1)v_{t-1} - (\lambda_1 - \lambda_2)v_{t-2} - \lambda_2 v_{t-3}. \tag{20}$$

The terms involving v represent the first difference of a moving average process.

A detailed preliminary examination of the serial correlation properties of income revealed that a second-order moving average model was appropriate. With moving average parameters ρ_1 and ρ_2, the stochastic model for the first difference of income is

$$\Delta y_t = \varepsilon_t + \eta_t - (1 - \rho_1)\eta_{t-1} - (\rho_1 - \rho_2)\eta_{t-2} - \rho_2 \eta_{t-3}. \tag{21}$$

Again, the terms involving η are the first difference of a moving average process. This model embodies the strong assumption that income is measured without error. A model augmented with an income measurement error would not be econometrically identified.

Although in the full life-cycle model the propensity to consume out of transitory income depends on age, in the results presented here, we approximate the full model by treating β as constant across the sample. We tried estimating the model separately for families with younger and older heads, but failed to find significant differences. Constancy of β across families has the substantial statistical advantage of making the simple moment matrix over families a sufficient statistic for all of the model.

We estimate the parameters of the model by maximum likelihood, under the assumption that ε, η, and v obey normal distributions. Maximum likelihood achieves the best fit of the variances and covariances predicted by the model to those found in the data; the likelihood function is a scalar measure of the fit. The key idea of our approach is to write out the formulas for the variances and covariances of the data implied by our theoretical model and then solve the resulting system of equations for the parameter estimates. To keep the exposition simple, we will first work out the case where transitory income and transitory consumption are not serially correlated ($\rho_1, \rho_2, \lambda_1$, and λ_2 are all taken as zero) and no consumers have advance information about income ($\phi = 0$). First, the variance of the first difference of income is

$$V(\Delta y_t) = \sigma_\varepsilon^2 + 2\sigma_\eta^2, \tag{22}$$

and the covariance of the first difference of income with its own lagged value is

$$\text{cov}(\Delta y_t, \Delta y_{t-1}) = -\sigma_\eta^2. \tag{23}$$

These two formulas give us estimates of the variance of the innovation in transitory income, σ_η^2, and of the variance of the increment in lifetime income, σ_ε^2. Next, the covariance of the first difference of consumption with its own lagged value is

$$\text{cov}(\Delta c_t, \Delta c_{t-1}) = -\sigma_v^2. \tag{24}$$

This gives us the last of the three variances, that of the innovation in transitory consumption, σ_v^2.

Information about the structural parameters α and β comes from the covariances of consumption and income. The contemporaneous covariance is

$$C_0 = \text{cov}(\Delta c_t, \Delta y_t) = \alpha\sigma_\varepsilon^2 + \alpha\beta\sigma_\eta^2, \tag{25}$$

and the covariance with future income is

$$C_1 = \text{cov}(\Delta c_t, \Delta y_{t+1}) = \alpha\beta\sigma_\eta^2. \tag{26}$$

Solving for α and β gives

$$\alpha = \frac{C_0 + C_1}{\sigma_\varepsilon^2}, \tag{27}$$

$$\beta = \frac{C_1}{C_0 + C_1}\frac{\sigma_\varepsilon^2}{\sigma_\eta^2}. \tag{28}$$

It is surprising that the contemporaneous covariance, C_0, has a central role in estimating the two propensities to consume, α and β. It is perhaps a little surprising that the covariance of the current change in consumption with the future change in income is equally important. The basic finding of the paper is that this covariance is small, so it is not plausible that consumers are excessively sensitive to transitory income. Why would we expect excessive sensitivity to show up as a strong negative correlation between the change in consumption and the future change in income?

Because those upward movements in consumption that are associated with the response to transitory income should be followed by a movement of income back toward normal in the following year. The first differences of income are negatively serially correlated (both in theory and in the data), so the correlation of the change in consumption and the subsequent change in income should reflect this negative serial correlation.

It might appear that the covariance of current consumption and lagged income could provide similar information. That covariance is also free of the effects of changes in the lifetime component of income. However, the optimal use of information hypothesized for consumers in the model implies that the covariance should be exactly zero; no information available in year $t - 1$ should help predict the change in consumption in year t. This is essentially the proposition formulated and tested in Hall (1978). The test will be carried out with the micro panel data of this study in a later section of the paper.

5.3   Advance Information about Income

Our data suggest that families have some information, but not full information, about next year's income innovations, ε_{t+1} and η_{t+1}, when they decide on this year's consumption, c_t. To incorporate this consideration, we introduce the future innovations into the consumption equation, weighted by a parameter, ϕ, which is interpreted as the fraction of advance information available to families. Because consumption is measured about a quarter of the way into the next year, a reasonable value for ϕ is around 0.25, and, indeed, our estimate is close to this value. The modified consumption equation is

$$\Delta c_t = \alpha\phi\varepsilon_{t+1} + \alpha(1 - \phi)\varepsilon_t + \alpha\beta\phi\eta_{t+1} + \alpha\beta(1 - \phi)\eta_t + \Delta c_t^S. \tag{29}$$

This model, or one observationally equivalent, can be derived from either of two sets of assumptions:

ASSUMPTION 1.   The annual income innovations ε_{t+1} and η_{t+1} are sums of, say, weekly innovations, and families have observed N of them when they make their consumption decisions; then $\phi = N/52$.

ASSUMPTION 2.   Families observe a noisy value of the future innovation, and ϕ is the coefficient applied to the noisy value in forming the best forecast of the actual value.

For the simple case where the transitory components are serially uncorrelated ($\rho_1 = \rho_2 = \lambda_1 = \lambda_2 = 0$), the cross-covariances the identify ϕ and the other key parameters are

$$C_0 = \text{cov}(\Delta c_t, \Delta y_t) = (1 - \phi)(\alpha\sigma_\varepsilon^2 + \alpha\beta\sigma_\eta^2), \tag{30}$$

$$C_1 = \text{cov}(\Delta c_t, \Delta y_{t+1}) = \phi(\alpha\sigma_\varepsilon^2 + \alpha\beta\sigma_\eta^2) - (1 - \phi)\alpha\beta\sigma_\eta^2, \tag{31}$$

$$C_2 = \text{cov}(\Delta c_t, \Delta y_{t+2}) = -\phi\alpha\beta\sigma_\eta^2, \tag{32}$$

If ϕ is zero, the solution of these equatons for α and β is the same as described in the previous section. If ϕ is one (complete advance informaton on income), the solution is the same, with C_1 taking the place of C_0 and C_2 taking the place of C_1. In general, to solve for all three parameters, we start with

$$\alpha = \frac{C_0 + C_1 + C_2}{\sigma_\varepsilon^2}. \tag{33}$$

The equations for β and ϕ are quadratic and it does not seem worth writing them out explicitly. Provided C_2 is negative (as it is in our data), the equations have a solution with ϕ between zero and one and a positive value of β.

In our model, we assume that families are homogeneous with respect to information about income—they all know a fraction ϕ of next year's income in making this year's consumption decisions. The covariances of this model are exactly the same as those for a model of heterogeneous families, where a fraction ϕ are fully aware of next year's income and the rest know nothing about it. The models are not completely the same, however. In the heterogeneous case, the distribution of Δc_t and Δy_t is not multivariate normal, but is a mixture of multivariate normals. Our estimates cannot be said to be maximum likelihood for the heterogeneous model.

The issue of advance information that might be available to market participants but not to the econometrician has also been considered in research on financial markets. The problem of the timing of the collection of data that obligates us to consider the issue here is not generally present in data on securities markets, but it may still be true that market participants have information in period t about what the econometrician labels an innovation in period $t + 1$. One supporting piece of evidence is the predicive power of stock prices for future movements of the money stock, found by Rozeff (1974) and Rogalski and Vinso (1977).

5.4   Estimation

Our bivariate model is

$$\Delta c_t = \alpha\phi\varepsilon_{t+1} + \alpha(1 - \phi)\varepsilon_t + \alpha\beta\phi\eta_{t+1} + \alpha\beta(1 - \phi)\eta_t + v_t$$
$$- (1 - \lambda_1)v_{t-1} - (\lambda_t - \lambda_2)v_{t-2} - \lambda_2 v_{t-3}$$

and

$$\Delta y_t = \varepsilon_t + \eta_t - (1 - \rho_1)\eta_{t-1} - (\rho_1 - \rho_2)\eta_{t-2} - \rho_2\eta_{t-3}. \tag{35}$$

Let x be the column vector of unobserved random variables,

$$x' = [\varepsilon_1, \ldots, \varepsilon_7, v_{-2}, \ldots, v_7, \eta_{-2}, \ldots, \eta_7]. \tag{36}$$

We assume that x is multivariate normal, with a diagonal covariance matrix, $\sum$ and variances

$$V(\varepsilon_t) = \sigma_\varepsilon^2, \tag{37}$$

$$V(v_t) = \sigma_v^2, \tag{38}$$

$$V(\eta_t) = \sigma_\eta^2. \tag{39}$$

Let z_i be the column vector containing the five differences of consumption and six first differences of income for family i:

$$z_i' = [\Delta c_1, \Delta c_2, \Delta c_3 + \Delta c_4, \Delta c_5, \Delta c_6, \Delta y_1, \Delta y_2, \Delta y_3, \Delta y_4, \Delta y_5, \Delta y_6]. \tag{40}$$

The model can be stated in the form

$$z_i = A x_i \tag{41}$$

(note that the third row of A has a special form) and z_i is multivariate normal. The covariance matrix of z_i is

$$\Omega(\theta) = A\Sigma A'. \tag{42}$$

Here θ is the vector of parameters,

$$\theta' = [\alpha, \beta, \lambda_1, \lambda_2, \rho_1, \rho_2, \sigma_\varepsilon^2, \sigma_v^2, \sigma_\eta^2, \phi]. \tag{43}$$

The log-likelihood of the sample is

$$L(\theta) = -\frac{N}{2} \log \det \Omega(\theta) - \frac{1}{2} \sum_{i=1}^{N} z_i' \Omega^{-1}(\theta) z_i \tag{44}$$

plus an inessential constant. We estimate θ by full numerical maximization of the likelihood. Its estimated covariance matrix is computed as the inverse of the information matrix, $\partial^2 L/\partial\theta\partial\theta'$. All computations were carried out by a program written by Bronwyn Hall, which uses analytical derivatives and the method of scoring.

5.5 Deterministic Components of Income and Food Consumption

The data whose variances and covariances are the starting point for the estimation process are the deviations of the changes in food consumption and income from deterministic paths. To form the deviations, we need estimates of the deterministic changes in income and consumption for each family in each year based on the family's characteristics in that year. We do this by assuming that the deterministic changes are functions of the family characteristics, then use ordinary least-squares regressions as follows: In the case of income, we regress the change in actual income on an intercept, the age of the household head, the age of household head squared, the change in the number of adults in the household, the change in the number of children in the household, and a linear time trend. Since food is a commodity whose relative price changed substantially over the period of our sample, we need to take account of the downward slope of families' demand functions. Thus the change in food consumption is regressed on the percentage change in the relative price of food (as measured by CPI components) as well as on the variables used in the income regressions. Results for the income and food consumption regressions are

ΔINCOME $= -433.96 + 33.23$ AGE $- 0.35$ AGE^2
$\qquad\qquad\quad$ (182.08)$\quad$ (7.89)$\qquad\quad$ (0.082)

$\qquad\qquad + 504.07\ \Delta$CHILD $+ 1535.06\ \Delta$ADULT
$\qquad\qquad\quad$ (30.55)$\qquad\qquad\qquad$ (40.99)

$\qquad\qquad - 53.44$ TIME,
$\qquad\qquad\quad$ (13.04)

13854 observations, $\qquad R^2 = 0.1383$, $\qquad$ standard error $= \$2606.4$;

$$\Delta \text{FOOD} = -96.67 + 3.89 \text{ AGE} - 0.045 \text{ AGE}^2$$
$$\phantom{\Delta \text{FOOD} = } (32.38) \quad (1.32) (0.014)$$

$$+ 166.56 \, \Delta \text{CHILD} + 242.46 \, \Delta \text{ADULT}$$
$$ (6.39) \phantom{\Delta \text{CHILD} } (8.72)$$

$$+ 2.00 \text{ TIME} - 440.62 \, \Delta \text{LOG PRICE},$$
$$ (2.65) \phantom{\text{TIME} } (244.85)$$

11545 observations, $\qquad R^2 = 0.1438,$ $\qquad$ standard error = \$542.02;

where ΔINCOME is the change in family income which is adjusted for income and FICA taxes and the cost of living, ΔFOOD is the change in family spending for food at home and in restaurants deflated into real terms, AGE is age of household head, AGE^2 is AGE squared, ΔCHILD is the change in the number of children in the household, ΔADULT is the change in the number of adults in the household, TIME is time trend ($1970 = 1 \cdots 1975 = 6$), ΔLOG PRICE is the change in the log of the relative price of food (measured by the food component of the CPI deflated by the overall CPI), and standard errors of the coefficients are in parentheses. The residuals from these regressions are then taken to be the deviations from the deterministic paths of changes in food consumption and income.

The specification of the food and income regressions make little difference to the results obtained for the stochastic model outlined above. For example, if the effect of family characteristics on the deterministic paths of income and food consumption are ignored—i.e., the change in the deterministic components is just assumed to be a constant—we find only very small differences in the estimates of the parameters of the stochastic model. For this reason, we believe that our implicit assumption that families have perfect foresight about the variables on the right-hand side of these regressions is an innocuous one, though clearly overly strong.

5.6 Results

The residuals from the preliminary regressions showed mild heteroskedasticity, especially in the first difference of consumption. Rather than complicate the model by introducing separate variances for each year, we simply transformed the covariance matrix of the residuals by dividing its rows and columns by suitable constants so that the variances of the first

differences of consumption were the same in all years (equal to the average
of the original data over the same years). We applied the same transformation to the income data. The spirit of this preliminary treatment of the data
is the same as conversion to a correlation matrix, but it preserves the units
of the structural parameters. Experiments with the alternative of estimating
variances gave essentially the same estimates of the structural parameters.

Estimation by maximum likelihood yielded the results shown in table
5.1. In summary, they show

1. The marginal propensity to consume lifetime income on food, α, is about
0.11, well under the average propensity in the raw data of 0.19.

2. The marginal propensity to consume out of transitory income relative
to the marginal propensity to consume out of lifetime income, β, is estimated as 0.29, somewhat above its theoretical value at reasonable discount
rates. The hypothesis of equal response to both components, $\beta = 1$, is
unambiguously rejected.

Table 5.1
Results for basic model

Parameter	Value (standard error)	Interpretation
α	0.107 (0.008)	Fraction of permanent income spent on food
β	0.292 (0.080)	Relative effect of innovation in transitory income compared to effect of innovation in lifetime income
ϕ	0.253 (0.058)	Fraction of information available in year t about income in year $t + 1$
λ_1	0.215 (0.014)	First moving average parameter for transitory consumption
λ_2	0.101 (0.017)	Second moving average parameter for transitory consumption
ρ_1	0.294 (0.021)	First moving average parameter for transitory income
ρ_2	0.114 (0.018)	Second moving average parameter for transitory income
σ_ε^2	1.49 (0.11)	Variance of innovation in lifetime income (thousands of dollars squared)
σ_r^2	0.158 (0.003)	Variance of innovation in transitory consumption
σ_η^2	3.41 (0.13)	Variance of innovation in transitory income

3. The fraction of information about next year's income, ϕ, is 0.25, in line with prior expectations.

Table 5.2 presents a reasonably complete accounting of the success of the model in fitting the pattern of covariation found in the data. For estimation of the key parameters α, β, and ϕ, the covariances of this year's change in consumption with this year's change in income, next year's change, and the subsequent year's change are the most important. All three parameters control the fitted value of the contemporaneous covariance— α and β make it larger, by making the change in consumption more sensitive to surprises in income, while ϕ makes it smaller, by making part of this year's change in consumption depend on next year's surprise in income. For the covariance with next year's income, β makes the fitted value more negative, for the reason explained earlier—if this year's consumption is sensitive to this year's transitory income, it will be negatively related to the change in next year's income when the transitory movement will probably be reversed. On the other hand, the fitted covariance is positively related to ϕ. If consumption is partly based on information about next year's surprise in income, this year's change will be positively correlated with next year's change in income. The fitted covariance of almost exactly zero represents cancellation of the two effects, since both β and ϕ

Table 5.2
Actual and fitted covariances

	Actual	Fitted
$\text{Var}(\Delta c)$	0.285	0.285
$\text{Var}(\Delta y)$	6.772	6.757
$\text{Cov}(\Delta c, \Delta y)$	0.234	0.200
$\text{Cov}(\Delta c, \Delta y_{+1})$	−0.004	0.003
$\text{Cov}(\Delta c, \Delta y_{+2})$	−0.021	−0.038
$\text{Cov}(\Delta c, \Delta y_{-1})$	−0.077	0.000
$\text{Cov}(\Delta c, \Delta c_{-1})$	−0.110	−0.106
$\text{Cov}(\Delta y, \Delta y_{-1})$	−1.948	−1.904
$\text{Cov}(\Delta y, \Delta y_{-2})$	−0.319	−0.339
$\text{Cov}(\Delta y, \Delta y_{-3})$	−0.383	−0.389

Notes: $\text{Var}(\Delta c)$ includes $\text{var}(\Delta c_3 + \Delta c_4)$: $\text{cov}(\Delta c, \Delta y)$ includes $\text{cov}(\Delta c_3 + \Delta c_4, \Delta y_3)$ and $\text{cov}(\Delta c_3 + \Delta c_4, \Delta y_4)$; $\text{cov}(\Delta c, \Delta y_{+1})$ includes $\text{cov}(\Delta c_3 + \Delta c_4, \Delta y_5)$; $\text{cov}(\Delta c, \Delta y_{+2})$ includes $\text{cov}(\Delta c_3 + \Delta c_4, \Delta y_6)$; $\text{cov}(\Delta c, \Delta y_{-1})$ includes $\text{cov}(\Delta c_3 + \Delta c_4, \Delta y_2)$, and $\text{cov}(\Delta c, \Delta c_{-1})$ includes $\text{cov}(\Delta c_3 + \Delta c_4, \Delta c_2)$ and $\text{cov}(\Delta c_5, \Delta c_3 + \Delta c_4)$.

are quite positive. The estimation process separates the effects of β and ϕ through the use of the covariance of this year's change in consumption with the change in income 2, 3, 4, and 5 years from now (of these, the closer ones are relatively more important). Under the hypothesis implicit in our model that consumers have no information about surprises in income more than one year in advance, the only explanation of the negative covariation of current consumption and future income operates through the sensitivity of consumption to transitory income, controlled by β. The estimation process chooses a substantially positive value of β in order to try to match the covariance of -0.021; the overstatement in the fitted value of -0.038 corresponds to understatements of some of the more distant covariances not shown in table 5.2.

An alternate explanation of the negative correlation of Δc_t and Δy_{t+2} is the possible inability of families to distinguish innovations in lifetime income from innovations in transitory income. If they cannot make the distinction at all, they are forced to react equally to both innovations, and so the estimate of β would be close to one. Our finding of a β above the level suggested by the theory may be a sign of limited information, not a sign of irrational behavior.

The only serious failure of the model revealed in Table 5.2 is its inability to explain the observed negative correlation of the current change in consumption and the lagged change in income. As we will show, the actual correlation is statistically significantly negative, yet the model holds that it should be exactly zero. The theoretical justification for the fitted correlation of zero is simple: Apart from its transitory component, consumption should respond only to new information, and lagged income cannot contain any new information. The next section of this chapter examines the apparent failure of this principle.

5.7   The Relation between Consumption and Lagged Income

The model has the straightforward implication that the simple regression of Δc_t on Δy_{t-1} should yield a coefficient on Δy_{t-1} of zero. Instead we find

$$\Delta c_t = 4.95 - 0.010\,\Delta y_{t-1},$$
$$\quad\;\;(6.16)\quad(0.002)$$

6926 observations,   standard error $= \$512$, $R^2 = 0.0028$.

Though the coefficient is quite small, it is statistically unambiguously negative. It would be uninteresting to conclude that the measurement error in Δc_t was negatively correlated with Δy_{t-1}, so we restrict our attention to explanations of a negative relation between the true change in consumption and the lagged change in income.

In this section we investigate the possibility that consumers are actually more sensitive to transitory income than is predicted by theory, but in a way not revealed in our examination of the joint behavior of Δc_t and Δy_t. The results in the previous section did not draw on the observed correlation between Δc_t and Δy_{t-1}—maximum likelihood is blind to covariances whose theoretical values are zero for all values of the parameters. An extended model proposed in Hall (1978) for a similar purpose can be used to examine the lagged relation. Suppose that a fraction $1 - \mu$ of consumption follows the life-cycle–permanent income theory, and the rest, a fraction μ, simply tracks current total income passively and so has an excessive sensitivity to transitory income. If all consumption were simply proportional to current income, the model would take the form

$$\Delta c_t = \alpha \Delta y_t + \Delta c_t^S$$

$$= \alpha \varepsilon_t + \alpha \eta_t - \alpha(1 - \rho_1)\eta_{t-1} - \alpha(\rho_1 - \rho_2)\eta_{t-2} - \alpha \rho_2 \eta_{t-3}$$

$$+ v_t - (1 - \lambda_1)v_{t-1} - (\lambda_1 - \lambda_2)v_{t-2} - \lambda_2 v_{t-3}. \tag{45}$$

The covariance of the change in consumption with last year's change in income implied by this model is

$$\operatorname{cov}(\Delta c_t, \Delta y_{t-1}) = -\alpha[(1 - \rho_1 + \rho_2)^2 - \rho_2]\sigma_\eta^2, \tag{46}$$

which is negative. The logic of the negative covariance is straightforward: If consumption tracks income, then a transitory rise in income this year will typically be followed next year by a decline in income and so also in consumption.

We estimated a model in which a fraction μ of consumption tracks income (measured as ϕ times next year's income plus $1 - \phi$ times this year's income), and a fraction $1 - \mu$ responds in the way suggested by the life-cycle–permanent income hypothesis. The model is

$$\Delta c_t = \alpha(\phi \varepsilon_{t+1} + (1 - \phi)\varepsilon_t) + \mu \alpha(\phi \Delta y_{t+1}^S + (1 - \phi)\Delta y_t^S)$$

$$+ (1 - \mu)\alpha \beta(\phi \eta_{t+1} + (1 - \phi)\eta_t) + \Delta c_t^S, \tag{47}$$

$$\Delta y_t = \varepsilon_t + \Delta y_t^S$$

$$= \varepsilon_t + \eta_t - (1 - \rho_1) - (\rho_1 - \rho_2)\eta_{t-2} - \rho_2 \eta_{t-3}. \tag{48}$$

The results of estimating the augmented model are as follows:

α 0.100   propensity to consume food out of lifetime income;
    (0.009)

β 0.174   propensity to consume out of a transitory increase in income
    (0.100)   relative to propensity to consume out of lifetime income;

ϕ 0.206   fraction of information available in year t about income in
    (0.058)   year $t + 1$;

μ 0.200   fraction of consumption direction proportional to current
    (0.065)   income.

The other parameter estimates are similar to their previous values. The new specification is about halfway successful in catching the covariance of this year's change in consumption with last year's change in income—the predicted value is -0.032 against the sample value of -0.077. Not surprisingly, the sensitivity of consumption to the innovation in transitory income is found to be smaller in the extended model, as the positive estimate the μ has taken over part of the job of explaining the positive contemporaneous covariation of consumption and income. Further, because μ and β are partly estimated from the same features of the data, joint estimation very substantially raises the sampling variation of the estimate of β, relative to the earlier results. The confidence interval for β now includes the theoretically expected value of about 0.10.

5.8   Concluding Remarks

According to our extended model, about 80% of consumption obeys the life-cycle–permanent income hypothesis. Consumption does not adjust in the same mechanical way to every change in income. Instead, consumers think about the source of a change in income and reach vigorously only to those changes that signal a major shift in economic well-being. But the data reject the strong hypothesis that all consumption is governed by the life-cycle–permanent income principle. This conclusion is independent of the model developed in this paper; it rests solely on the rather general principle that changes in consumption should not be predictable on the basis of information available to the household. The negative relation between the lagged change in income and the current change in consumption is consistent with constrained consumption behavior for about 20% of consumption. We are able to distinguish this symptom of inability (or unwillingness) to borrow and lend from the type of behavior characteristic of consumers who simply face high effective interest rates. The data show signs of both influences. Consumption is somewhat more sensitive to current income than it would be in an economy where every consumer borrowed and lent freely at the Treasury bill rate. Still, it is much less sensitive than in an economy where no consumer ever borrowed or lent at all.

The overwhelming bulk of the movements in income that give rise to our inference from the data are unrelated to the behavior of the national economy; most are probably highly personal. It is purely an inference, though a reasonable one in our opinion, that households respond to income fluctuations attributable to the business cycle or to countercyclical tax policy in the same way they respond to purely personal income fluctuations. Our results cast doubt on the wisdom of tax policies to manipulate aggregate demand by changing disposable income. If, as the results indicate, most consumers react only to the new information about their permanent incomes conveyed by the announcement of a tax change, then policymakers face the complicated task of inferring consumers' interpretation of the announcement. Lucas (1976) has pointed out the obstacles to policy evaluation in these circumstances.

Our evidence and conclusions refer specifically to food consumption and more generally to the consumption of nondurables. Nothing in our work describes the response of consumer purchases of durable goods to changes in income. Our finding that food consumption behaves as if constraints on borrowing were relatively unimportant does not rule out important constraints for the acquisiton of durables. The sensitivity of durables purchases to transitory income is very definitely a topic for further research, where some of the techniques devloped in this paper may be helpful.

Notes

This research was supported by the National Science Foundation through a grant to the National Bureau of Economic Research. We are grateful to numerous colleagues, especially Ariel Pakes, for helpful comments. The research reported here is part of the NBER's research program in Economic Fluctuations. Any opinions expressed are those of the authors and not those of the National Bureau of Economic Research.

1. These tests and the empirical work here are closely related to the large body of research on the behavior of financial markets under rational expectations. Consumption is the analogue of a stock price, for example, and income is the analogue of earnings per share of the corporation issuing the stock. Our test of the predictive power of lagged income is the analogue of similar tests for market efficiency in the stock market, in the sense of the unpredictability of changes in stock prices from publicly available information (Fama 1970 and Mishkin 1978). In contrast to our findings for consumption, the hypothesis of unpredictability is generally supported by the data for security markets. The technique developed in this paper could be transplanted directly to securities markets to answer such questions as: Do stock prices overreact to current movements of earnings? Do market participants have advance information about earnings?

2. Note that this budget constraint requires that y_t not include the expected return on nonhuman wealth, A_t. Flavin (1981) discusses why the failure to recognize this can lead to errors.

3. The survey interviewers were instructed to estimate income and food consumption when an interviewee was unsure of the questions concerning these items. We excluded all of the cases where this imputation was done.

4. Here, we are neglecting the issue of advance information about income; the appropriate modifications are presented in the next section.

References

Ando, A., and F. Modiglian. 1963. "The 'Life-Cycle' Hypothesis of Saving: Aggregate Implications and Tests." *American Economic Review* 53: 55–84.

Bewley, T. 1976. "The Permanent Income Hypothesis: A Theoretical Formulation." Department of Economics, Harvard University, September.

Eisner, R. 1969. "Fiscal and Monetary Policy Reconsidered." *American Economic Review* 59: 897–905.

Fama, E. F. 1970. "Efficient Capital Markets: A Review of Theory and Empirical Work." *Journal of Finance* 25: 383–417.

Flavin. M. 1981. "The Adjustment of Consumption to Changing Expectations About Future Income." *Journal of Political Economy* 89: 974–1009.

Friedman, M. 1957. *A Theory of the Consumption Function*. Princeton, New Jersey: Princeton University Press.

Hall, R. E. 1978. "Stochastic Implications of the Life-Cycle–Permanent Income Hypothesis: Theory and Evidence." *Journal of Political Economy* 86: 971–987 (chapter 4 in this volume).

Hall, R. E. 1980 "Consumption and Real Interest Rates."

Lucas, R. E. "Econometric Policy Evaluation: A Critique." In *The Phillips Curve and Labor Markets*. Carnegie-Rochester Conference Series on Public Policy, 1, ed. K. Brunner and A. H. Meltzer. Amsterdam: North-Holland, pp. 19–46.

Mayer, T. 1972a. "Tests of the Permanent Income Theory with Continuous Budgets." *Journal of Money Credit and Banking* 6: 757–778.

Mayer, T. 1972b. *Permanent Income, Wealth and Consumption*. Berkeley: University of California Press.

Mishkin, F. S. 1978. "Efficient-Markets Theory: Implications for Monetary Policy." *Brookings Papers on Economic Activity* 2: 707–752.

Muth, J. F. 1960. "Optimal Properties of Exponentially Weighted Forecasts." *Journal of the American Statistical Association* 55: 299–306.

Okun, A. 1971. "The Personal Tax Surcharge and Consumer Demand." *Brookings Papers on Economic Activity* 1: 167–204.

Rogalski, R. J., and J. D. Vinso 1977. "Stock Returns, Money Supply and the Direction of Causality." *Journal of Finance* 32: 1017–1030.

Rozeff, M. S. 1974. "Money and Stock Prices: Market Efficiency and the Lag in the Effect of Monetary Policy." *Journal of Financial Economics* 1: 245–302.

Tobin, J., and W. Dolde 1971. "Wealth, Liquidity and Consumption." In *Consumer Spending and Monetary Policy: The Linkages*. Federal Reserve Bank of Boston, 99–146.

Yaari, M. 1976. "A Law of Large Numbers in the Theory of Consumer's Choice under Uncertainty." *Journal of Economic Theory* 12: 202–217.

6 Intertemporal Substitution in Consumption

One of the important determinants of the response of saving and consumption to the real interest rate is the elasticity of intertemporal substitution. That elasticity can be measured by the response of the rate of change of consumption to changes in the expected real interest rate. A detailed study of data for the twentieth-century United States shows no strong evidence that the elasticity of intertemporal substitution is positive. Earlier findings of substantially positive elasticities are reversed when appropriate estimation methods are used.

A higher expected real interest rate makes consumers defer consumption, everything else held constant. The magnitude of this intertemporal substitution effect is one of the central questions of macroeconomics. If consumers can be induced to postpone consumption by modest increases in interest rates, then (1) movements of interest rates will make consumption decline whenever other components of aggregate demand rise—total output will not be much influenced by changes in those components; (2) the deadweight loss from the taxation of interest is important; (3) the burden of the national debt or unfunded social security is relatively unimportant; and (4) consumption will move along with real interest rates over the business cycle, to name four of the many issues that rest on the intertemporal substitutability of consumption.

This chapter estimates parameters of the representative individual's utility function rather than parameters of the consumption function or savings function. As Lucas (1976) has pointed out, there may not be anything that can properly be called a consumption or savings function: the relation between consumption, income, and interest rates depends on the wider macroeconomic context and may not be stable over time, even though consumers are always trying to maximize the same utility function. The techniques of this chapter are more robust with respect to this kind of instability than standard econometric models of consumption and savings.

The essential idea of the chapter is that consumers plan to change their consumption from one year to the next by an amount that depends on their expectations of real interest rates. Actual movements of consumption differ from planned movements by a completely unpredictable random variable that indexes all the information available next year that was not incorporated in the planning process the year before. If expectations of real interest rates shift, then there should be a corresponding shift in the rate of

Reprinted with permission from *Journal of Political Economy*, vol. 96, no. 2, pp. 339–357, © 1988 by The University of Chicago.

change of consumption. The magnitude of the response of consumption to a change in real interest expectations measures the intertemporal elasticity of substitution. All this is set up in a formal econometric model in which the assumptions are formalized and the estimation techniques rigorously justified.

Over the postwar period, there have been downward and upward shifts in the expected real return from common stocks, Treasury bills, and savings accounts, three of the investments that govern the real interest rate for consumers. Over the same period, there have been only small shifts in the rate of growth of consumption. Consequently, all the estimates presented in this paper of the intertemporal elasticity of substitution are small. Most of them are also quite precise, supporting the strong conclusion that the elasticity is unlikely to be much above 0.1 and may well be zero.

6.1 Theory of the Consumer under Uncertain Real Interest Rates

Finance theory has examined the role of the consumer in an economy with one or more securities with stochastic returns. Breeden (1977, 1979) was the pioneer in what has become known as the consumption capital asset pricing model. Hansen and Singleton (1983) provide an application of the model to macroeconomic consumption data. Mankiw, Rotemberg, and Summers (1985) have extended the model to include labor supply. The basic model of the joint distribution of consumption and the return earned by one asset that has emerged from that research is the following: The joint distribution of the log of consumption in period t, c_t, and the return earned by the asset from period $t - 1$ to period t, r_{t-1}, is normal with a covariance matrix that is unchanging over time. The means obey the linear relation

$$\bar{c}_t = \sigma \bar{r}_{t-1} + c_{t-1} + k. \tag{1}$$

That is, the expected change in the log of consumption is parameter, σ, times the expected real return plus a constant.

The simplest rationalization for this model of the joint distribution of the two variables is based on the hypothesis that the consumer maximizes the expected value of an intertemporally separable utility function

$$\sum e^{-\delta t + [1 - (1/\sigma)]c_t}. \tag{2}$$

For the purposes of deriving the joint distribution of consumption growth and the real return, it is not necessary to make specific assumptions about the market setting of the maximization. At one extreme, the consumer could face a full set of markets in contingent commodities, and then the budget constraint would say that the sum of all the consumer's demands for the contingent claims valued at market prices would equal his endowment. At the other extreme, the consumer could be Robinson Crusoe, with a single risky investment in a real asset. Then the budget constraint would say that his holdings of the real asset could never be negative. For a further discussion of this point, see Grossman and Shiller (1982).

In any case, one of the many choices facing the consumer is to spend a little less in year $t - 1$, invest the savings in one asset, and spend the stochastic proceeds in year t. Suppose that a unit investment in year $t - 1$ has the stochastic return $e^{r_{t-1}}$ in year t. The first-order condition for the deferral of a small amount of consumption from period $t - 1$ to period t, considered from the point of view of a consumption decision made in $t - 1$, is

$$E_{t-1}[e^{r_{t-1}-(1/\sigma)c_t} - e^{\delta-(1/\sigma)c_{t-1}}] = 0. \tag{3}$$

Equation 3 is the precise mathematical formulation of the principle that the marginal rate of substitution should equal the ratio of the prices of present and future consumption. Under uncertainty, it is not true that the expected marginal rate of substitution should equal the expected price ratio (the discount function). Rather, the appropriate discount rate is the risk-adjusted one described by the first factor in equation 3; it is the expectation of the product of the discount function and the marginal stochastic utility next period. This expression is related to the "consumption beta" of modern finance theory.

The reallocation condition of equation 3 is the generalization of the proposition investigated in my earlier paper (Hall 1978) that marginal utility should be a trended random walk when real interest rates are constant over time. Further progress in translating the reallocation condition into consequences for observed variables requires assumptions about the distributions of the random influences. A set of assumptions related to those introduced by Breeden (1977) seems a natural approach. First, assume that the real interest rate, r_{t-1}, conditional on information available in year $t - 1$, obeys the normal distribution with mean $\bar{r}_{t-1}$. Because interest rates as they are defined in this paper can be indefinitely negative, the normal distribution is a natural assumption. Second, assume that the consumer's rule for processing new information about Income and interest rates makes the distribution of consumption log-normal, conditional on information available last year; that is, log c_t is normal with mean $\bar{c}_t$. Because the new information arriving in year t has a bearing both on the actual return to investments maturing in t and on the consumer's long-term well-being estimated in that year, the two random variables r_{t-1} and c_t will be correlated.

Applying the intertemporal allocation condition under the assumptions of log-normality gives the relation between the expected value of the log of consumption in period t given consumption in period $t - 1$ and the mean of the distribution of the real interest rate:

$$\bar{c}_t = \sigma \bar{r}_{t-1} + c_{t-1} + k. \tag{1}$$

Here k is a constant that depends on the variances and covariance of z, r, and c. I will assume that it does not change significantly over time.

This condition says that the mean level of consumption in period t generated by the consumer's choice as of period $t - 1$ is the level of consumption chosen for period $t - 1$ plus a constant plus an adjustment positively related to the mean of the real interest rate. A high value of σ means that when the real interest rate is expected to be high, the consumer will actively defer consumption to the later period.

The condition is a constraint on the consumption rule. It says that an optimal rule will wind up choosing a level of consumption in period t, after the new information becomes available, whose mean obeys this restriction. The condition is not a complete description of consumption behavior under uncertainty. It does not describe the actual amount by which consumption changes when new information about income or asset returns becomes available.

The actual log of consumption in period t, c_t, differs from the mean, $\bar{c}_t$, by a completely unpredictable surprise, which I will call ε_t. By the hypotheses already stated, ε_t is a normal random variable. The two equations of interest can be put in the form of a bivariate regression:

$$c_t = \sigma \bar{r}_{t-1} + c_{t-1} + k + \varepsilon_t, \tag{4}$$

$$r_{t-1} = \bar{r}_{t-1} + v_t. \tag{5}$$

The random variable v_t also has the normal distribution.

If the expected real interest rate $\bar{r}_{t-1}$ is observed directly, then the key parameter σ can be estimated simply by regressing the change in the log of consumption on the expected real rate. That regression also has the property that no other variable known in period $t - 1$ belongs in the regression. The strong testable implication of the theory is that the mean of the rate of growth of consumption is shifted only by the mean of the real interest rate. Information available in year $t - 1$ is helpful in predicting the rate of growth of consumption only to the extent that it predicts the real interest rate. This testable implication is the logical extension of the one derived in my earlier paper (Hall 1978) under constancy of real interest rates. In that case, no variable known in year $t - 1$ should help predict the rate of growth of consumption.

6.1.1 Interpretation of the Parameter σ

In the model of finance theory, based on the maximization of the expected value of the intertemporally additive utility function of equation (6.2), the parameter σ is interpreted as the reciprocal of the coefficient of relative risk aversion. However, σ is the intertemporal elasticity of substitution as well. The two parameters are assumed to be reciprocals of one another. If consumers are highly risk averse, they must have low intertemporal substitution as well. For the purposes of this reseach, it would be desirable to eliminate this automatic connection between intertemporal substitution and risk aversion. The empirical finding that intertemporal substitution is weak or absent does not contradict any widely held beliefs about consumer behavior. But the corresponding conclusion that the coefficient of relative risk aversion is close to infinity is incompatible with the observed willingness of consumers to take on risk. Hence, it is desirable to show that the finding of this paper has no automatic bearing on risk aversion.

It is a topic of active research in the theory of the consumer as to how to characterize preferences about uncertainty and intertemporal choice. It is apparent that the relationship between the rate of growth of consumption and the expected real interest rate is governed by the intertemporal substitution aspect of preferences. That is, the parameter σ in equation 1 is on its face the intertemporal elasticity; it is literally the elasticity of the consumption ratio to the corresponding relative price. Under certainty, where only intertemporal substitution has a role, equation 1 would hold for an intertemporally separable utility function with a constant elasticity of substitution, σ.

With the maximization of the expected value of the utility function 2, it is unarguably the case that $1/\sigma$ is the coefficient of relative risk aversion as well. However, recent work has shown that equation 1 does not reveal the coefficient of relative risk aversion under less restrictive assumptions about preferences. The earliest research on finding a clean separation between intertemporal substitution and risk aversion appears in a characterization of preference orderings with only two time periods by Selden (1978) in what he calls the ordinal certainty equivalence (OCE) framework. The OCE setup departs from expected utility but retains additive separability. In the OCE framework, the relation between consumption growth and expected real interest reveals just the intertemporal elasticity of substitution and says nothing about the coefficient of relative risk aversion. Selden lets one concave function describe risk aversion in the second period. With it, risk aversion has the effect of reducing uncertain future consumption to its certainty equivalent. Then a second utility function describes intertemporal substitution between current consumption and the certainty equivalent of future consumption. Under the assumption that both utility functions have the constant-elastic form, and the same log-normal assumptions about the interest rate and future consumption, the OCE framework gives rise to exactly equation 1 (for details, see Hall 1985). It is an unambiguous conclusion that the intertemporal elasticity of substitution alone controls the relation between consumption growth and the expected real interest rate. Unfortunately, the OCE framework does not generalize in any known way to more than two periods (see Johnsen and Donaldson 1985).

More recently, partly in response to remarks in earlier versions of this paper, a number of authors have developed representations of intertemporal preferences under uncertainty that depart from expected utility in a way originally proposed by Kreps and Porteus (1978). Attanasio (1987), Epstein and Zin (1987a, 1987b), Weil (1987), and Zin (1987a, 1987b) have all shown that, under suitable assumptions, the Kreps-Porteus setup implies that the coefficient σ is the intertemporal elasticity of substitution and not the reciprocal of the coefficient of relative risk aversion.

In the framework developed here, the bivariate relation between consumption and real interest rates does not necessarily reveal anything about risk aversion. Estimation of the risk aversion parameter would be possible in a multivariate system that considered the real returns to two or more assets. Then the magnitudes of the risk premiums together with the correlations of the returns with consumption would provide estimates of the coefficient of relative risk aversion.

In this chapter I will refer to the parameter σ as the intertemporal elasticity of substitution; I do not think this interpretation is at all controversial. Readers who have a strong prior belief that the utility function is additively separable and that consumers follow the principle of maximizing expected utility will also interpret σ as the reciprocal of the coefficient of relative risk aversion. Others, such as myself, will avoid drawing any conclusions about risk aversion from the results presented here.

6.1.2   Relation to Hansen and Singleton

Hansen and Singleton (1983) studied the joint distribution of the rate of growth of consumption and asset returns in the conventional expected intertemporal utility framework. They do not mention intertemporal substitution in their discussion at all. They identify the single critical parameter they estimate as the coefficient of relative risk aversion. Their statistical model is the same as the one derived here. Their estimation technique, based on maximum likelihood in a bivariate system, examines the relation between the rate of change of consumption and expected real asset returns and interprets the coefficient as the reciprocal of the coefficient of relative risk aversion. In their framework, as I mentioned above, the coefficient is also the intertemporal elasticity of substitution. The argument offered here suggests that Hansen and Singleton's estimated coefficient may not be informative about risk aversion. However, I do not offer any evidence on this question one way or the other.

Hansen and Singleton (1983), and Grossman and Shiller (1982) before them, are on firm ground in treating the differences in returns among assets as revealing something about risk aversion. Indeed, Hansen and Singleton's rejection of the cross-equation restrictions in a model combining consumption growth with returns on multiple assets may occur because the intertemporal elasticity of substitution is different from the reciprocal of the coefficient of relative risk aversion.

6.2   Expectations of the Real Interest Rate

I take two approaches to the measurement of the expected real interest rate. First, I study changes in consumption over a period for which survey data on expected price changes are available. The expected real interest rate is the market nominal rate for an instrument of suitable term, adjusted for taxes, less the expected rate of change of the price level. Real returns from the stock market can also be used in this framework because survey data on expected nominal stock prices are available.

The second approach relates the conditional mean of the real interest rate, $\bar{r}_{t-1}$, to observed variables known to consumers at the time that they choose c_{t-1}. Recall that $\bar{r}_{t-1}$ is the mean of the subjective distribution for the real interest rate held by the typical consumer at the time consumption decisions are made for year $t - 1$. A specification for expectations that has been employed frequently in macroeconomic models derived from rational expectations and, in particular, underlies the recent work of Hansen and Singleton is derived as follows. Let the mean of the subjective distribution be a linear combination of observed variables,

$$\bar{r}_{t-1} = x_{t-1}\beta, \tag{6}$$

and suppose that the coefficients, β, are known in advance. Under this specification, the complete model of expectations and consumption becomes a simple application of bivariate regression with parameter constraints across the equations. AltHernatively, the same estimation technique can be thought of as instrumental variables applied to the consumption equation, with the determinants of the expected real rate as the instruments. The second interpretation is the one adopted in this paper, in which all estimates are obtained by instrumental variables except when expectations are observed directly.

6.3   Time Aggregation

The basic equation for the rate of change of consumption,

$$\Delta c_t = \sigma \bar{r}_{t-1} + k + \varepsilon_t, \tag{7}$$

refers to consumption in discrete time. From the derivation in section 1, it is also apparent that it applies to observations on the instantaneous flow of consumption measured at two points of time in a setup in which time is measured continuously. However, it does not correctly characterize the behavior of time averages of consumption. If c_t is the average flow of consumption over an interval of continuous time, then the relation of its rate of change to the real interest rate is more complex. My discussion will note the difference between time aggregation of the level of consumption and aggregation of its logarithm. The difference is trivial for consumption because it changes so little during any given year.

As with other aggregation problems in econometrics, time aggregation for the left-hand variable causes only mild problems. If the right-hand variable is observed continuously, or at least quite frequently, then the aggregation of the left-hand variable in effect defines an appropriate way to aggregate the right-hand variable. The problem of time aggregation becomes much more difficult if only a time average of the right-hand variable is available (Grossman, Melino, and Shiller 1985). However, in the present case, interest rates and rates of inflation are measured monthly or more frequently over the whole time span for which any data at all are available for consumption, so the time aggregation problem is readily soluble.

Suppose that only a time average of consumption is observed, say once a year. Each month, the expected real interest rate is known; call it $\bar{r}_{t,m}$ with t the year and m the month. There is an unobserved $c_{t,m}$ each month, and it evolves as

$$\Delta c_{t,m} = \sigma \bar{r}_{t,m-1} + \varepsilon_{t,m}. \tag{8}$$

Now write out $c_{t-1,m}$ and $c_{t,m}$ as increments over the initial value $c_{t-1,1}$. Note that, to a close approximation,

$$c_t = \frac{1}{12} \sum c_{t,m} + \log 12. \tag{9}$$

Then a little manipulation shows that the change in aggregate consumption is

$$\Delta c_t = \frac{1}{12} \sum_{m=1}^{12} (m-1)(\sigma \bar{r}_{t-1,m-1} + \varepsilon_{t-1,m})$$

$$+ \frac{1}{12} \sum_{m=1}^{12} (12 - m + 1)(\sigma \bar{r}_{t,m-1} + \varepsilon_{t,m}). \tag{10}$$

Define the time aggregates of the expected real interest rate and the random element as

$$\bar{r}_{t-1} = \frac{1}{12} [\Sigma(m-1)\bar{r}_{t-1,m-1} + \Sigma(12 - m + 1)\bar{r}_{t,m-1}], \tag{11}$$

$$\varepsilon_t = \frac{1}{12} [\Sigma(m-1)\varepsilon_{t-1,m} + \Sigma(12 - m + 1)\varepsilon_{t,m}]. \tag{12}$$

Then the relation among the time aggregates is

$$\Delta c_t = \sigma \bar{r}_{t-1} + \varepsilon_t. \tag{13}$$

Two properties of the aggregate random element ε_t call for note. First, as Working derived in a famous paper (1960), ε_t is not white noise; rather, it obeys a first-order moving average process with serial correlation 0.25. Second, ε_t is likely to be correlated with r_{t-1} or with its determinants or instruments, even if these variables are uncorrelated at the monthly level.

The combination of serial correlation in the residuals and endogenous instrumental variables calls for an estimator designed to deal with these circumstances. Hayashi and Sims (1983) have provided what seems to be the most suitable estimator for this problem. They propose that the data on the left- and right-hand variables undergo a preliminary transformation that yields a scalar covariance matrix for the disturbances. However, the transformation must also preserve the timing conditions that make the instruments and the transformed disturbances orthogonal. The standard autoregressive transformation destroys the timing conditions. On the other hand, an autoregressive transformation that subtracts future rather than past values will preserve the timing conditions and accomplish the necessary transformation. Application of the Hayashi-Sims estimator in the present case is particularly easy because the time-series process for the disturbances is prescribed by theory and does not need to be estimated in a preliminary stage. The process is first-order moving average with a parameter of 0.27. The corresponding autoregressive transformation can be closely approximated as

$$\Delta \bar{c}_t = \Delta c_t - 0.27 \Delta c_{t+1} + 0.07 \Delta c_{t+2}. \tag{14}$$

This is the first two terms of the infinite autoregressive representation of the first-order moving average process. The same transformation is applied to the real interest rate variable. Then the instrumental variables estimator is applied to the transformed variables, using untransformed lagged variables as instruments. Hayashi and Sims show that the resulting estimates are consistent and that the standard estimate of the covariance matrix of the estimates is also consistent.

In estimating the time-aggregated Euler equation, the timing of the instruments turns out to be critical. If the data measured the instantaneous flow of consumption at two isolated points, any variable known at the time that c_{t-1} was chosen would be eligible as an instrument. However, when

c_{t-1} is an annual average, it is apparent that any variable measured during calendar year $t - 1$ can be correlated with the disturbance ε_t. For annual data, the most recent permissible instrument is one measured in December of year $t - 2$. Annual aggregates for year $t - 2$ and earlier are usable, but not those for year $t - 1$. The most recent variables eligible as instruments are the change in annual log consumption in year $t - 2$, the level of the average real return over year $t - 2$, and nominal return in December of year $t - 2$.

6.4   Data

Following are brief definitions of the data series used in this study: $c_t = \log$ of real consumption of nondurables (not including services) in year, quarter, or month t, from the U.S. National Income and Product Accounts; the data are available monthly from 1959, quarterly from 1947, and annually from 1919 (for derivation before 1929, see Hall 1986); $r_t =$ realized real return after taxes on an investment in the Standard and Poor's (S&P) 500 stock portfolio, liquidated at a later date corresponding to the consumption variable, or realized real return after taxes from a savings account earning the regulated passbook interest rate or realized real return after taxes from holding a sequence of four 90-day Treasury bills over the year; $h_t = \log$ os the S&P 500 index of share prices, deflated; $d_t =$ dividend yield of the S&P 500; $z_t =$ nominal yield of Treasury bills, discount basis; $q_t =$ nominal passbook interest rate in the third quarter; $p_t = \log$ of the implicit deflator for consumption of nondurables (used as a deflator for all deflated variables).

After-tax magnitudes were calculated using the effective marginal rate under the federal personal income tax from Barro and Sahasakul (1983). The full nominal amount of dividends and interest was assumed to be taxed at this effective marginal rate. Capital gains and losses were assumed to be untaxed on the grounds that the combination of low statutory rates, taxation only at realization, and forgiveness of accrued gains at death makes the effective rate close to zero. All data for the study are available from the author on an IBM diskette.

6.5   Summary of Results

Following is a brief summary of the various attempts I have made to estimate the intertemporal elasticity of substitution by estimating the relationship of the rate of change of consumption to expected real interest rates.

The first set of results uses inflation and stock price expectations recorded in the Livingston survey (see section 6.6). In this work, the expected real return is measured directly and the elasticity of substitution estimated by simple regression. For real returns in the stock market, the results are informative: the elasticity of substitution is close to zero and the estimate has a small standard error. For savings accounts and Treasury bills, the estimates are almost useless because of large standard errors. In these cases, the lack of variation in the expected real return makes it difficult to estimate the elasticity.

A second set of results uses annual changes in consumption starting in 1924. The real return on Treasury bills is aggregated from monthly data, as suggested in section 6.3. Because this technique uses a longer span of data and uses all the data for each year, the standard error of the estimate of the intertemporal elasticity is much smaller. The point estimate of the elasticity is negative. All positive values lie outside the 95% confidence interval.

A third set of results reconciles the findings of this chapter—that the intertemporal elasticity is around zero—with Hansen and Singleton's finding of large positive elasticities. The difference comes from their choice of a time period for estimation and from their use of instruments that are correlated with the innovation in the real return.

A fourth set of results examines Summers's (1982) findings of intertemporal elasticities of around one, using quarterly postwar data. Again, use of an appropriate estimator reverses his conclusion.

My overall conclusion from all four sets of results is that the evidence points in the direction of a low value for the intertemporal elasticity. The value may even be zero and is probably not above 0.2.

Before plunging into formal econometric results, I think it is useful to indicate why the data point toward the answer that pervades the results of this paper, namely, that the intertemporal elasticity of substitution is small. Some simple facts about the data are apparent just by taking averages over 5-year intervals. The averaging removes most of the random expectation errors but turns out to leave a good deal of variation in the real interest rate. Figure 6.1 shows the real after-tax return on Treasury bills and the rate of change of consumption for intervals from 1921 through 1940 and 1946–83 (the last interval is only 3 years long).

Percent change in consumption

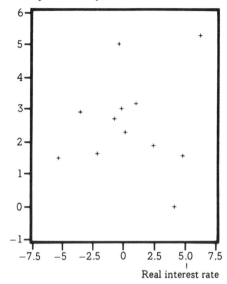

Figure 6.1
Five-year averages of the real return on Treasury bills (horizontal axis) and the rate of
change of consumption (vertical axis), 1921–1940 and 1946–1983

Except for three of the observations, the rate of change of consumption
is close to its average value of a little below 3% per year. When consumption
was near average, however, the real interest rate varied from −5% to +5%.
The only observation combining a high real interest rate and rapid consumption growth was for 1921–25, in the upper right-hand corner. The
other observation with high consumption growth was for 1936–40, when
the real interest rate was almost exacly zero. The period 1931–35 had a
high real interest rate and slightly negative consumption change. As a
general matter, figure 6.1 makes a fairly strong case that periods of high
real interest rates have not typically been periods of high consumption
growth. Rather, consumption growth has generally stuck fairly close to its
average value no matter what has happed to real interest rates.

6.6   Results Based on the Livingston Survey

Each November, Joseph Livingston asks a panel of economists to predict
the values of a long list of economic variables for the following June. Among

the variables are the consumer price index and the S&P 400 stock price index. From these, it is possible to construct three measures of expected real returns that are relevant for consumers.

Treasury bills. The starting point is the market value of a bill maturing in June as reported in November. All elements of the expected real rate are known except for the marginal tax rate, which is highly predictable. I computed the expected real return as

$$r = \log\left[\frac{1 - (7/12)mz}{1 - (7/12)z} - \frac{p_N}{p_J}\right]. \tag{15}$$

Here z is the nominal return measured in discount form at an annual rate (as a decimal), m is the marginal tax rate, p_N is the known price level in November, and p_J is the expected price level in June.

Savings accounts. Nominal bank rates, q, are not entirely known in advance but are highly predictable. I compute the expected real after-tax return as

$$\log\left(\{e^{(7/12)q} - m[1 - e^{(7/12)q}]\}\frac{p_N}{p_J}\right). \tag{16}$$

Stocks. I treat the dividend yield, d, as known and use the survey data for the expected share price. The expected real after-tax return is

$$\log\left\{\left[\frac{7}{12}(1 - m)d + \frac{h_J}{h_N}\right]\frac{p_N}{p_J}\right\}. \tag{17}$$

Here h_N is the known stock price index in November and h_J is the expected index for the following June.

The dependent variable, the log of the change in consumption per capita, is constructed to match the Livingston data as closely as possible. Monthly data on consumption in November and June are divided by monthly estimates of the U.S. population.

The results from the regression of the log change in consumption on these three measures of the expected real return are the following (standard errors are in parentheses):

Security	Estimate of σ	Standard error	Durbin-Watson
Treasury bills	0.346 (0.337)	0.0169	2.13
Savings accounts	0.271 (0.330)	0.0170	2.17
Stocks	0.066 (0.050)	0.0166	2.36

The results for Treasury bills and savings accounts are hardly conclusive. The variation in the expected real returns over the (twenty-four 7-month periods in the data is inadequate to provide any useful information about the elasticity of substitution, σ. But for the stock market, the results are conclusive. The estimate of σ is close to zero and the standard error is small as well. The confidence interval for σ excludes all values that correspond to strong intertemporal substitution.

6.7   Results from Annual Data with Consistent Time Aggregation

Annual averages of consumption are available starting just after World War I. Monthly data on the realized return on Treasury bills can be calculated for the same period. Aggregation of the real return data to annual rates, as described in section 6.3, makes it possible to estimate the intertemporal elasticity of substitution from a much longer historical record with much more variance in expected real returns. The estimate of the intertemporal elasticity of substitution obtained by applying the Hayashi-Sims estimator with the annual log of the change in consumption per capita as the dependent variable and realized real returns as the independent variable, with the change in consumption 2 years earlier, the realized real return 2 years earlier, and the nominal bill rate in December 2 years ago as instruments, for the years 1924–40 and 1950–83, is

estimate of σ: -0.40 D-W: 2.09;   SE: 2.5%.
                  (0.20)

The finding of a negative value of the intertemporal elasticity of substitution was not sensitive to the choice of instruments as long as endogenous variables from year $t - 1$ were excluded. Separate estimates for the pre- and postwar periods showed that the estimate was somewhat negative in the earlier period and positive for the later period. However, the pooled estimate clearly rejects all positive values of σ. It simply cannot be said that the relation between the real return and the rate of change of consumption supports strong intertemporal substitution. Of course, the finding of a negative estimate of σ cannot be taken literally, since it implies nonconcave utility. Rather, the conclusion I draw is that the case for a significantly positive value of σ cannot be made in this framework.

6.8   Results Based on Recent Monthly Data

Hansen and Singleton (1983) obtained results with monthly data that can be interpreted as evidence of large values for σ. Although I have not attempted to reproduce their results exactly, simple instrumental estimates do give high estimates of σ, especially over the particular time period they studied. For example, for data from October 1959 through December 1978, with the real rate lagged 1–6 months and the rate of change of consumption lagged 1, 2, and 3 months as instruments, I obtain

estimate of σ: 0.98   D-W: 2.59;   SE: 0.81%.
                    (0.33)

The real return is computed from monthly averages of daily data. Following Hansen and Singleton, I have not made adjustments in the real return to take account of time aggregation nor have I used the Hayashi-Sims estimator. Incorporating data through December 1983, I get a somewhat lower value with the same procedure:

estimate of σ: 0.48   D-W: 2.64;   SE: 0.79%.
                    (0.22)

Hansen and Singleton's use of the immediately lagged change in log consumption as an instrument does not give rise to a consistent estimate of σ when the dependent variable is the change in a time aggregate. Section 3 showed that last year's change in consumption depends on some of the same random disturbances as this year's change. The most recent change in consumption admissible as an instrument is the one lagged 2 years.

Because data on the price level are compiled no more frequently than monthly, it is not possible to apply the full apparatus developed earlier in this paper for monthly data. However, it is possible to come close. A good approximation to the correct time aggregate of the real return on Treasury bills can be computed, with respect to the change in consumption between last month and this month, by using the simple average of the Treasury bill yields in each of the months, adjusted for taxes, less a moving average of price changes. The moving average gives a weight of 0.125 to next month's price change, 0.75 to this month's, and 0.125 to last month's. These weights can be derived by combining a simple interpolation formula with the aggregation process derived in section 6.3. Then the Hayashi-Sims estimator can be applied. Because the computed real return uses an additional future month's price data, the earliest value that can be used as an instrument is from 3 months ago. However, the observed nominal yields on Treasury bills 2 and 3 months ago can be used as instruments. Making all these changes, including dropping Δc_{t-1} from the list of instruments, further reduces the estimate of σ:

estimate of σ: -0.03 D-W: 3.00;   SE: 0.91%.
                    (0.38)

For the stock market, use of recent monthly data does not change the conclusion reached by Hansen and Singleton and the earlier results in this paper that the estimate of the elasticity is reliably low:

estimate of σ: 0.03   D-W: 3.02;   SE: 0.90%.
                    (0.10)

Large fluctuations occurred over the period from 1959 through 1983 in the expected real return from the stock market, not matched by corresponding changes in the rate of change of consumption. The monthly results for the stock market strongly confirm the results from 7-month changes in the earlier study with the Livingston data.

All the results for monthly data show negative serial correlation of the first difference of consumption after the small adjustments for the effects of changes in the expected real interest rate and after the orthogonalizing transformation. This negative serial correlation suggests that there is a transitory element in monthly consumption that is not accounted for by the model. Similar but weaker evidence is found for quarterly data but not for annual data.

6.9   Results Based on Postwar Quarterly Data

Summers (1982) presents results to support the view that the intertemporal elasticity of consumption is substantial. In a subsequent paper (Summers

1984), he has cited his findings in making a case for the interest elasticity of saving: "available evidence tends to suggest that savings are likely to be interest elastic. I find in the more reliable estimates in my working paper [Summers 1982] values of the intertemporal elasticity of substitution which cluster at the high end of the range Evans and I considered [above one]. Similar estimates are found ... by Hansen-Singleton. Where investigators find low estimates of intertemporal elasticity of substitution, it is usually because of the difficulty in modelling *ex ante* rates of return on corporate stock" (p. 252).

I have not tried to duplicate Summers's findings exactly. With postwar quarterly data on consumption and time averages of the real after-tax yield on Treasury bills computed as described in section 6.3, I have obtained the following estimate of σ using the same inappropriate instruments as Summers, namely, the real yield, the inflation rate, and the rate of change of consumption dated $t - 1$ and $t - 2$, and without transforming for the serial correlation induced by time aggregation:

estimate of σ: 0.34   D-W: 1.95;   SE: 0.87%.
                  (0.13)

However, use of the Hayashi-Sims estimator and deletion of the instruments known to be correlated with the disturbance reverses the finding of an unambiguously positive σ:

estimate of σ: 0.10   D-W   2.49;   SE: 0.88%.
                  (0.23)

6.10   Conclusions

My investigation has shown little basis for a conclusion that the behavior of aggregate consumption in the United States in the twentieth century reveals an important positive value of the intertemporal elasticity of substitution. All investigators have agreed that the covariation of stock market returns and consumption did not suggest that consumption rises more rapidly in times of high expected real returns in the stock market. Earlier evidence based on interest-bearing securities such as Treasury bills had suggested values of σ as high as one. However, use of appropriate estimation techniques taking account of time aggregation reverses this finding. Moreover, extension of the investigation to prewar years and to data from the past few years strengthens the evidence that periods of high expected real interest rates have not been periods of rapid growth of consumption.

Note

This research was supported in part by the National Science Foundation and is part of the research program in economic fluctuation of the National Burreau of Economic Research. All opinions expressed are mine alone. I thank John Caskey and Valerie Ramey for outstanding assistance and Sanford Grossman, Peter Hammond, Lars Hansen, James Heckman, Kenneth Judd, Stephen LeRoy, and Kenneth Singleton.

References

Attanasio, Orazio P. 1987. "A Note on the Interpretation of the Time Series Behaviour of Consumption and Asset Returns." Working Paper no. 1015. London: London School Econ., Centre Labour Econ.

Barro, Robert J., and Sahasakul, Chaipat. 1983. "Measuring the Average Marginal Tax Rate from the Individual Income Tax." *J. Bus.* 56 (October): 419–452.

Breeden, Douglas T. 1977. "Changes in Consumption and Investment Opportunities and the Valuation of Securities." Ph.D. dissertation, Stanford Univ.

Breeden, Douglas T. 1979. "An Intertemporal Asset Pricing Model with Stochastic Consumption and Investment Opportunities." *J. Financial Econ.* 7 (September): 265–296.

Epstein, Larry G., and Zin, Stanley E. 1987a. "Substitution, Risk Aversion, and the Temporal Behaviour of Consumption and Asset Returns. I: A Theoretical Framework." Working Paper no. 8715. Toronto: Univ. Toronto.

Epstein, Larry G., and Zin, Stanley E. 1987b. "Substitution, Risk Aversion, and the Temporal Behaviour of Consumption and Asset Returns. II: An Empirical Analysis." Discussion Paper no. 698. Kingston, Ont.: Queen's Univ.

Grossman, Sanford J.; Melino, Angelo; and Shiller, Robert J. 1985. "Estimating the Continuous-Time Consumption-based Asset Pricing Model." Working Paper no. 1643. Cambridge, Mass.: NBER, June.

Grossman, Sanford J., and Shiller, Robert J. 1982. "Consumption Correlatedness and Risk Measurement in Economies with Non-traded Assets and Heterogeneous Information." *J. Financial Econ.* 10 (July): 195–210.

Hall, Robert E. 1978. "Stochastic Implications of the Life Cycle–Permanent Income Hypothesis: Theory and Evidence." *J. P. E.* 86 (December): 971–987.

Hall, Robert E. 1985. "Real Interest and Consumption." Working Paper no. 1694. Cambridge, Mass.: NBER, August.

Hall, Robert E. 1986. "The Role of Consumption in Economic Fluctuations." In *The American Business Cycle: Continuity and Change*, edited by Robert J. Gordon. Chicago: Univ. Chicago Press (for NBER).

Hansen, Lars Peter, and Singleton, Kenneth J. 1983. "Stochastic Consumption, Risk Aversion, and the Temporal Behavior of Asset Returns." *J. P. E.* 91 (April): 249–265.

Hayashi, Fumio, and Sims, Christopher A. 1983. "Nearly Efficient Estimation of Time Series Models with Predetermined but Not Exogenous, Instruments." *Econometrica* 51 (May): 783–798.

Johnsen, Thore H., and Donaldson, John B. 1985. "The Structure of Intertemporal Preferences under Uncertainty and Time Consistent Plans." *Econometrica* 53 (November): 1451–1458.

Lucas, Robert E., Jr. 1976. "Econometric Policy Evaluation: A Critique." In *The Phillips Curve and Labor Markets*, edited by Karl Brunner and Allan H. Meltzer. Carnegie-Rochester Conference Series on Public Policy, vol. 1. Suppl., *J. Monetary Econ.*

Mankiw, N. Gregory; Rotemberg, Julio J.; and Summers, Lawrence H. 1985. "Intertemporal Substitution in Macroeconomics." *Q.J.E.* 100 (February): 225–251.

Selden, Larry. 1978. "A New Representation of Preferences over Certain × Uncertain' Consumption Pairs: The 'Ordinal Certainty Equivalent' Hypothesis." *Econometrica* 46 (September): 1045–1060.

Summers, Lawrence H. 1982. "Tax Policy, the Rate of Return, and Savings." Working Paper no. 995. Cambridge, Mass.: NBER, September.

Summers, Lawrence H. 1984. "The After-Tax Rate of Return Affects Private Savings." *A.E.R. Papers and Proc.* 74 (May): 249–253.

Weil, Phillipe. 1987. "Non-expected Utility in Macroeconomics." Manuscript. Cambridge, Mass.: Harvard Univ.

Working, Holbrook. 1960. "Note on the Correlation of First Differences of Averages in a Random Chain." *Econometrica* 28 (October): 916–918.

Zin, Stanley E. 1987a. "Aggregate Consumption Behaviour in a Life Cycle Model with Non-additive Recursive Utility." Discussion Paper no. 693. Kingston, Ont.: Queen's Univ.

Zin, Stanley E. 1987b. "Intemporal Substitution, Risk, and the Time Series Behaviour of Consumption and Asset Returns." Discussion Paper no. 694. Kingston, Ont.: Queen's Univ.

7 Survey of Research on the Random Walk of Consumption

No specialty in macroeconomics has been more profoundly influenced by the rational expectations revolution than has the study of consumption. From the early 1950s, when the life cycle–permanent income hypothesis came to dominate the profession's thinking about consumption, until the late 1970s, the consumption field was largely dormant. In the following decade, however, a substantial upsurge of new work has occurred. Although almost all of the new work embodies the hypothesis of rational expectations, much more has been added to our thinking than just the simple idea that consumers make consumption plans on the basis of all available information about future income.

My survey of this work will start with the initial impact of rational expectations—the development of the Euler equation characterization of optimal consumption behavior and the empirical tests of it. Tests have been applied by a number of authors using data for the United States and for a number of other countries. Roughly speaking, the Euler equation says that consumption should evolve as a random walk; that is, the change in consumption should not be predictable. The empirical work testing this proposition says, in sum, that consumption is fairly close to a random walk, but certain variables have enough predictive power that the hypothesis is rejected in formal statistical tests.

One interesting branch of the ensuing research has asked whether the predictability of the change in consumption can be explained by the inability of consumers to borrow when income is temporarily low. The investigation of "liquidity constraints" has occupied quite a number of investigators, most of whom have reached the conclusion that liquidity constraints do help to explain aspects of the data not explained by the simple rational expectations life-cycle–permanent income hypothesis. They typically find that most of the movements of consumption are consistent with the simple model; only a minority of consumers are constrained.

Another branch has sought to explain departures from the simple random walk by examining the implications of the durability of consumption goods. Durability turns out to compete with liquidity constraints, in that models containing both features do not rely very heavily on liquidity constraints to explain the predictability of consumption.

The third branch of the literature I shall examine considers a more refined version of the Euler equation. Theoretically, changes in expected

Reprinted with permission from "Consumption," in Robert J. Barro (ed.), *Modern Business Cycle Theory* (Cambridge, MA: Harvard University Press, 1989), pp. 153–177.

real returns should influence the rate of change of consumption. When asset markets offer high returns, consumers should defer consumption. That is, the rate of growth of consumption of individual households should be positively correlated with the expected return. Rejection of the simple random walk model might be the result of this correlation. However, the aggregation of interest-rate effects is a complicated issue; there is no simple relation between expected real returns and the rate of growth of aggregate consumption.

There are some important topics related to consumption that I have excluded from this discussion. In particular, the literature stimulated by Robert Barro's work on Ricardian equivalence is outside my domain. On this, see Bernheim's (1987) survey and synthesis.

7.1 Rational Expectations and the Euler Equation

Work on consumption from the time of Keynes's *General Theory* focused on the development of a consumption function, that is, a structural relation between income (and possibly and interest rate) and consumption. Friedman's permanent income hypothesis and Modigliani's life-cycle hypothesis were seen as suggestions about the way that income variables might enter the consumption function. The main point was that temporary changes in income should have less impact on consumption than should permanent changes. Probably the most impressive evidence on the point was in Friedman's examination of cross-sectional data on family income and consumption. When it came to building a consumption function, however, Friedman and his followers (such as Darby (1972)) made consumption a distributed lag of current and past income. Muth (1960) had shown that a geometric distributed lag was optimal under rational expectations only with a certain special stochastic process for income, but the consumption function literature did not pursue this point until many years later. In aggregate U.S. data, the distributed lag from income to consumption had a peculiar feature—either most of the weight applied to current income or the lag came out almost infinitely long.

Ando and Modiglian's empirical consumption function (1963) took a more structural view of expectations. They reasoned that the Unemployment rate was an additional variable that the public might consider in deciding whether the current level of real income was representative of its permanent level.

The opening shot in the rational expectations revolution was Robert Lucas's (1976) famous critique of econometric policy models that was presented in 1973. The models he criticized consisted of sets of structural equations. One of the three structural equations he found wanting was the consumption function. And his criticism was profound. It was not that the typcial consumption function was misspecified. Rather, he said, there is no such thing as a consumption function. There is a structural relation between permanent income and consumption, but the consumption function asserts a structural relation between observed income and permanent income, and there is no reason to expect a stable relation of that type. Changes elsewhere in the economy—for example, in stabilization policy—could alter the optimal way for a consumer to make an inference about permanent income from observed income. Development of consumption functions has little purpose. In particular, a model for policy analysis based on a consumption function is self-defeating.

Although Lucas was scornful of existing econometric policy evaluation models, his message was not completely destructive of all model-building or empirical research. There are structural relationships in the economy, but the consumption function is not among them. For consumption, the structural relation, invariant to policy interventions and other shifts else-where in the economy, is the intertemporal preference ordering. The view of consumption that flowed from Lucas's work is that today's level of consumption is the level chosen by consumers to maximize expected life-time utility, given all available information about current and future in-come and prices. The consumer uses all available knowledge about the behavior of other actors in the economy, including the government, in processing the information.

Lucas's critique of the consumption function was overshadowed by his critique of the Phillips curve, where he generalized and formalized a point made very effectively several years earlier by Friedman (1968). The next step in the development of the rational expectations view of consumption was Hall's (1978) test of a general implication of Lucas's view. Hall neither tried to repair the traditional consumption function nor tried to estimate the deep parameters of utility. Rather, he formulated a simple empirical test of the idea that consumers maximize the expected value of lifetime utility subject to an unchanging real interest rate. The basic idea is to look at the Euler equation describing the optimal behavior of such a consumer. The Euler equation characterizes the equality of the marginal rate of substitution between consumption this year and consumption next year to the relative price of the two. That relative price is simply the present discounted cost of a unit of future consumption. Mathematically, the consumer seeks to maximize

$$E_t \sum_s \left(\frac{1}{1+\delta}\right)^s u(c_{t+s})$$

$$\text{s.t.} \sum_s \left(\frac{1}{1+r}\right)^s (c_{t+s} - w_{t+s}) = A_t.$$

The notation is

    E_t = mathematical expectation conditional on all information in t;

    δ = rate of subjective time preference;

    r = real rate of interest, a constant over time;

  $u(\cdot)$ = one-period utility function, strictly concave;

    c_t = consumption;

    w_t = earnings from sources other than savings;

    A_t = assets apart from human capital.

On the possible relaxation of assumption of intertemporal separability, see Browning (1986b). Derivation of results with constant expected real interest rates in general equilibrium appears in Christiano, Eichenbaum, and Marshall (1987).

The Euler equation expressing the equality of the marginal rate of substitution to the price ratio is

$$E_t u'(c_{t+1}) = \frac{1+\delta}{1+r} u'(c_t).$$

That is, marginal utility next year is expected to be the same as marginal utility this year, except for a trend associated with the constant rate of time preference δ and the constant real interest rate r. Another way to express the same idea is

$$u'(c_{t+1}) = \frac{1+\delta}{1+r} u'(c_t) + \varepsilon_t.$$

Here ε is a random variable whose expectation at time t (when consumption c_t is being chosen) is zero. In particular, ε is uncorrelated with $u'(c_t)$, so this equation is a regression. If the functional form of $u(\cdot)$ were known, this equation could be the basis of a test of optimization. For the optimizing consumer, no variable observed in year t would receive a nonzero coefficient if added to the equation. If a variable were found that helped predict next year's marginal utility and if that variable were known to the consumer at the time c_t was chosen, then the consumer would be shown to have failed to optimize.

Hall's original work did not try to make use of information about the functional form of utility function. Instead, he argued that the Euler equation could be approximated closely by assuming a quadratic utility function, in which case it could be written as

$$c_{t+1} = \lambda c_t + \varepsilon_t.$$

In this framework, the basic test of optimization involves placing additional variables on the right-hand side and computing the t- or F-test for their exclusion.

Chang (1987) considered the issue of when simple random-walk relations hold exactly. Zeldes (1986) computed consumption functions numerically with nonnegativity constraints and concluded that the quadratic specification can be misleading in some circumstances.

Hall found that lagged real disposable income had little predictive power for consumption; the hypothesis that only, c_t helped predict c_{t+1} among variables dated t and earlier was accepted. However, he showed that the Euler-equation restriction was rejected for the stock market. The recent change in the real value of the stock market has statistically significant predictive power for the future change in consumption.

Flavin (1981) examined the relation between income and consumption in the rational expectations framework and found sufficient predictive power to reject the strict optimization hypothesis. Her theoretical work involved the development of an explicit structural consumption function, based on the hypothesis that real income obeys a stable stochastic process. Thus her model itself is subject to Lucas's criticism, which points out that the stochastic process of income is a result of the interaction of all the actors in the economy and is not a deep structural characteristic of the consumer alone. However, her test turned out to be identical to the type of test proposed by Hall. She found rejection of optimization because she included more lagged values of income than Hall had tried and because of a few other minor changes.

Flavin's structural model enabled her to interpret her findings quantitatively. In her results, the parameter describing the excess response of consumption to the contemporaneous change in income is about 0.36. She pointed out that the relatively small values of coefficients found by Hall on lagged income in the reduced-form consumption regression signify much larger structural coefficients. As a general matter, Flavin found even more evidence than did Hall to reject the pure optimization model with a constant real interest rate.

Goodfriend (1986) pointed out that Flavin's procedure rests on the hypothesis that aggregate income is immediately observable If, instead, there is a one-quarter lag before aggregate income becomes public, one would expect rejection roughly along the lines found by Flavin.

Mankiw and Shapiro (1985b) criticized Flavin's work on the grounds that her detrending procedure would induce the finding of excess sensitivity even if it were absent from the original data. They considered an example in which income is a random walk. Optimal consumption is also a random walk. Hall's test applied to the original data will not reject optimization. However, with detrended data, income and consumption will be cyclical and will flunk Hall's test. They noted that Flavin's test is indecisive in the original data, because income is essentially a random walk before detrending.

Stock and West (1987) challenged Mankiw and Shapiro's interpretation of excess sensitivity as arising from a spuriously detrended random walk. They argued that by detrending a random walk with drift, Flavin induced a change in the large sample distribution from a normal to a nonstandard distribution of the type associated with an ARIMA process with unit roots. Using theoretical results of Sims, Stock, and Watson (1987), they noted that, in contrast, Hall's original tests based on lagged consumption were valid even with preliminary detrending of the data. The key difference between Hall's and Flavin's procedures is that Hall included lagged consumption as a regressor, whereas Flavin did not. Stock and West presented the results of Monte Carlo experiments to support their argument, which is otherwise based on asymptotic theory. In addition, results obtained by Deaton (1986) cast doubt on the hypothesis that the bias identified by Mankiw and Shapiro can fully explain the finding of excess sensitivity of consumption to income.

Deaton's work also casts doubt on the likelihood of success of models that try to fit a stochastic process to income and then infer the appropriate response of consumption to the innovations in that process. He noted that a nonstationary process for real income—specifically, a first-order autoregressive process in the first difference—seems to provide a reasonable description of the income process. But for that process, the observed response of consumption to an income innovation is much too small rather than too big. Subtle differences in the income process have major implications for the consumption response. Accordingly, results obtained within a restricted class of income processes may not give reliable statistical tests of the hypothesis of excess sensitivity. Campbell and Deaton (1987) pursued the idea and fitted a number of low-order ARIMA models of income. Most of them have the property that the innovation in consumption should have a larger variance than the innovation in income. They also reached the same conclusion by examining the autocorrelations of income. However, both of their procedures are biased toward the conclusion that consumption is excessively smooth, so their findings are inconclusive.

West (1986) used a variance bounds technique to examine the question of the relative variabilities of consumption and income. He concluded that the evidence is ambiguous, thogh possibly it favors excess smoothness of consumption. In a related paper, Christiano (1987) found that small influences on consumption through intertemporal substitution associated with variations in real returns could explain an apparent excess smoothness of consumption.

Nelson (1987) reexamined Hall's original empirical results and Flavin's later work. He argued that a more reasonable approximation could be achieved by assuming logarithmic utility and a long-normal distribution for later consumption given earlier consumption. He demonstrated that the current change in income is a statistically significant predictor of the coming change in consumption in that framework. Nelson also confirmed that Flavin's strong results on excess sensitivity may be the result of her procedure for detrending the data.

Jacobson (1981) showed that measures of consumer attitudes had predictive power even in the presence of the stock-market value included in Hall's original study.

Miron (1986) showed that the results obtained by Flavin and others rejecting the simple random-walk hypothesis could be reversed by using seasonally unadjusted data and on explicit model of seasonal effects rather than by using seasonally adjusted data.

Kormendi and LaHaye (1986) carried out tests of the explanatory power of lagged income changes for the current change in consumption for a panel of thirty countries. They failed to reject the hypothesis of no explanatory power for the panel as a whole. Using Flavin's approach, they found that consumption appears to be undersensitive to changes in permanent income.

7.1.1   Time Aggregation

Evans (1982), Christiano (1984), and others have pointed out that the data employed to test the Euler equation are time averages, whereas the theory deals with consumption chosen at isolated points in time. Working (1960) derived the time-series properties of a time average of a random walk. The first difference of the time average is a first-order moving average process with a serial correlation of about 0.25. Tests of the Euler equation can be modified to take account of this property—it implies particular coefficients for lagged consumption and invalidates the most recent observation on real income in the test regression. Hall (1988) treated the time aggregation problem at some length, but neither he nor any other author has repeated the Euler equation tests to take account of time aggregation. Estimation problems with time-aggregated data are discussed in detail in Hansen and Singleton (1986).

7.1.2   Findings of Countries Other than the United States

Daly and Hadjimatheou (1981) repeated Hall's basic Euler-equation test using data for the United Kingdom. They found substantial predictive power for lagged disposable income and lagged liquid assets; they rejected the exclusion of those variables from the Eular equation unambiguously. Their work was criticized by Cuddington and Hurd (1981) on the grounds that they presented only the final results of an extensive search for successul predictors. However, Muellbauer (1983) found a similar rejection for the United Kingdom using only consumption lagged once and income lagged once and twice.

Cuddington (1982) examined Canadian data and found significant predictive power for real money balances, real private wealth, real GNP, and the unemployment rate.

Johnson (1983) rejected the Euler equation optimization condition with Australian data. He found predictive power for certain measures of lagged income and the unemployment rate.

7.1.3   Findings in Cross-Sectional Data

In principle, variations in income and consumption experienced by individual families should provide more powerful tests of models of consumption. However, some of the advantages of the proliferation of observations available in cross sections are lost because of measurement problems. In the United States, for example, there is no body of data that reports on the total consumption of families in successive years. Much of the resesarch on U.S. data has been done with data on income and food consumption from the Panel Study of Income Dynamics.

Hall and Mishkin (1982) examined this body of data within the framework of a rational expectations theory of consumption. Their model hypothesizes that consumption at the level of the individual family has a transitory measurement error or other source of noise not explained by the theory. In the presence of such an error, the simple regression test of the Euler equation is restricted: it must impose a unit coefficient on lagged consumption and cannot use further lags of consumption as candidates for failure of the hypothesis of unpredictability. Hall and Mishkin regressed the first difference of food consumption on the lagged change in income and found a coefficient of -0.10 with a standard error of 0.002. The rejection of optimization is strong statistically, although the magnitude of the departure from the theoretical value of zero is small.

Hall and Mishkin also estimated a structural model of consumption similar to Flavin's. Their model departs from hers in two ways. First, it permits current consumption to respond to the immediate future innovation in income. This modification is suggested by the timing of the data and also by the possibility that familes have some advance information about income changes. The results confirm that such advance information is available to families. Second, the model permits a fraction of consumption to move in proportion to actual current income instead of permanent income. If a fraction of the sample is liquidity constrained, their income will move in this way. The results suggest that about 20% of consumption is linked to current rather than permanent income. With these two modifications, the model is successful in explaining the entire pattern of covariances of income and food consumption found in the data.

Hayashi (1985) studied a panel of Japanese households in a similar framework. In addition to food consumption, the panel reports data on four other categories of consumption. Hayashi found that lagged income has significant predictive power for the change in consumption, in contradiction to the Euler equation characterization of optimization. He formulated a more general model to explain the predictive power of income, which included the possibility of liquidity constraints and also the possibility that consumption in one period provides satisfaction in succeeding periods. He incorporated the latter effect by making the utility function depend on a distributed lag of past expenditures. His results show that the durability of consumption is an important part of the explanation of the failure of the simple Euler equation. After taking account of durability, he found a sharp estimate that 15% of households are liquidity constrained.

Altonji and Siow (1987) considered the problem of errors in measuring income in panel studies. They show that income measurement errors are important quantitatively but that the generally favorable findings in panel studies of the life-cycle–permanent income model are confirmed when the errors are considered explicity.

Working with highly detailed data from a Norwegian panel, Mork and Smith (1986) found results generally favorable to the life cycle–permanent income model.

7.1.4   Restrictions Imposed by the Rational Expectations–Permanent Income Model on the Joint Behavior of Income and Consumption

Sargent (1978) was the first to investigate the problem of formulating optimal consumption behavior as a restriction on a general time-series model of income and consumption. However, as pointed out by Flavin (1981), Sargent's version of the permanent income model did not take account of the fact that current saving finances future consumption. As a result, the restrictions he derived and tested were not a satisfactory characterization of optimal consumption. Flavin derived the restrictions implied by the standard permanent income model. The cross-equation restrictions on the coefficients of lagged variables turn out to be exactly those tested by Hall (1978)—the exclusion of all variables other than lagged consumption in the autoregressive representation for consumption. She showed that there are no restriction operating across the coefficients of the two autoregressions. However, if one interprets the univariate time-series model of income literally, in the sense that no lagged variable other than income is useful in forecasting income, the model also implies an important restriction on the covariance matrix of the innovations of consumption and income. That matrix is singular; the two innovations are proportional to one another and the theory relates their constant of proportionality to the coefficients of the income process. Sargent did not consider the restrictions on the covariance matrix. Flavin argued that the singularity should not be expected in actual data, where a more elaborate model would be appropriate. In that mode, consumers use information to forecast future income that is not conveyed by the current and past levels of income. Then the innovation in consumption is not perfectly correlated with the innovation in income, nor does theory prescribe the numerical relation between the two innovations. If people respond to the information contained in other variables in addition to income, the measured correlation of the innovations in income and in consumption should be less than one. It is tempting to interpret the residual in an income autoregression as proportional to the innovation in permanent income. However, if people respond to variables in addition to the ones in the econometrician's right-hand variables, the residual in an income equation will be an error-ridden measure of the innovation in permanent income. Flavin's analysis of the covariance matrix of the income and consumption residuals indicates that the magnitude of the measurement error is far from negligible.

The issue of the singularity of the covariance matrix of a set of variables under certain information assumptions with rational expectations was also considered at a more general level by Sargent and Hansen (1981).

John Campbell (1986) considered by the restrictions imposed by optimal consumption behavior on a three-variable system comprising consumption, labor income, and capital income (the latter defined as the constant expected real interest rate times the level of assets). He showed that the restrictions implied by theory can be stated as parameter restrictions on a vector autoregression. The first restriction is that capital income evolves according to the intertemporal budget constraint with constant expected real interest rate (the actual return ex post can be random). This restriction is a statement about the technology, not about consumption behavior.

The second restriction is that either the change in consumption, or, equivalently, the statistic

$$s_t - \Delta x_t - (1 + r)s_{t-1}$$

(where s_t is saving and x_t is labor income) is unpredictable. This statistic is the innovation in consumption plus the innovation in capital income, so it is unpredictable for essentially the same reasons that the change in consumption is unpredictable.

Campbell's test is close to a test of the unpredictability of consumption changes and has the same partial equilibrium character because he does not test the constancy of expected real rates. The advantage of his framework is that it can be used to assess the quantitative importance for savings behavior of deviations from the permanent income theory.

Campbell also made the interesting observation that the level of saving can be written as the present discounted value of expected future declines in noncapital income. That is, the permanent income model explains saving only through the income-smoothing motive. In the model, saving is positive only when income exceeds its permanent level and is consequently expected to decline in the future. In fact, average saving is higher than the model predicts.

The movements of saving also differ somewhat from those of the optimal forecast of the decline in labor income, but the two variables have about the same standard deviations. Campbell argued that if consumption were excessively sensitive to income, then saving would have a lower standard deviation than would the optimal forecast. He concluded that the failure of the permanent income model should not be described as excess sensitivity.

Campbell and Clarida (1986) obtained results for Canada and Britain that are quite similar to those for the United States.

7.1.5 Liquidity Constraints

The notion that the sensitivity of consumption to income is greater than that predicted by the permanent income hypothesis has long been associated with the idea that households are unable to dissave during periods of abnormally low income. Instead of continuing a normal level of consumption by drawing down financial assets or borrowing, they must reduce consumption. Such households face liquidity constraints because they do not hold liquid assets or collateral suitable for borrowing.

Hayashi (1987) has provided a very complete survey of the literature on liquidity constraints. My remarks here are selective.

Muellbauer (1983) and Zeldes (1985) developed the theory of the response of consumers to liquidity constraints within the framework of the rational expectations–permanent income model. As they noted, it is an oversimplification to say that liquidity-constrained consumers simply spend all of their disposable income. Rather, the liquidity constraint has a shadow price that functions as an interest rate. In circumstances where an unconstrained consumer would maintain consumption by dissaving, a consumer influenced by liquidity constraints will behave as if he faced a higher interest rate. The consumer will substitute away from current consumption because it is, in effect, more expensive. Although an Euler equation can be derived for the consumer facing a liquidity constraint, it includes a term involving the shadow price of the constraint. The determination of that shadow price involves a consideration of the entire intertemporal planning problem of the consumer and does not decompose in a simple way. Because the current shadow price is almost certainly correlated with current and past income, the simple Euler equation proposition of unpredictable changes in consumption does not hold for the liquidity-constrained consumer.

Runkle (1983) and Zeldes examined liquidity constraints in panel data for individual households. They applied the simple Euler equation test in log form; that is, they tested the hypothesis that the rate of growth of consumption is unpredictable except for a term involving market interest rates. They showed that for households with low net worth, who are candidates for liquidity constraints, the hypothesis is rejected. Runkle found that the rate of growth of consumption is positively related to net worth in families with assets below $1500, whereas Zeldes found that consumption growth is negatively related to real disposable income. The latter finding was also reported by Hall and Mishkin (1982) and other authors who interpreted their findings as supporting liquidity constraints but did not develop a formal model of the effect of the constraints.

Flavin (1985) examined the issue of liquidity constraints in time-series data in an extended version of her earlier model. She considered two explanations of her earlier finding that the innovation in consumption is excessively sensitive to the innovation in income. First, consumers may be myopic—that is, they may behave as if they faced extremely high interest rates at all times. Second, some consumers at some times may face liquidity constraints. She noted that the two alternative explanations can be distinguished by studying the relation of excess sensitivity to variables that measure the incidence of liquidity constraints. For this purpose, she used the unemployment rate. In the null hypothesis derived from the rational expectations–permanent income hypothesis, the unemployment rate helps predict future income but has no direct influence on consumption in the absence of liquidity constraints. Flavin found that when the unemployment rate is included in the model as an additional variable to forecast income but is constrained to have no direct effect on consumption, the excess sensitivity of consumption to current income is large and statistically significant, as before. However, when the unemployment rate, interpreted as an indicator of liquidity constraints, is permitted to have a direct impact on consumption, the measured excess sensitivity of consumption to income falls substantially in magnitude and becomes insignificant. Because of the high degree of correlation between the unemployment rate and income, the empirical results do not provide clear-cut, conclusions, but Flavin interpreted the results as providing some support for a role of liquidity constraints.

Muellbauer and Bover (1986) developed a more elaborate model of liquidity constraints in time series data and concluded that the model provides a good description of U.S. data.

Browning (1987) tested for liquidity constraints in a novel way. Under the assumptions that married couples plan to have children sooner or later and that there is not shift of preferences for drinking and smoking as a result of the arrival of children, life-cycle theory predicts that there should be no change in alcohol and tobacco consumption when children arrive. British panel data support this proposition.

7.1.6   Durable Goods

At the most basic level, the theory of durables consumption is no different from the theory of nondurables consumption. Households consume a flow of services from durables and that flow should be determined in the same way as the flow of other types of consumption. However, a number of authors have gone beyond this simple statement to build and estimate models that deal with the joint behavior of income and the acquisition of stocks of durables.

Mankiw (1982) developed the most basic model in a time series setting. He noted that the stock of durables should evolve according to the same Euler equation as the flow of consumption of nondurables. If the deterioration of the stock of durables occurs at a constant rate, the purchases of durables should obey a first-order autoregressive, first-order moving average process; the parameter of the moving average process depends only on the rate of deterioration. He obtained strong rejection of that hypothesis. He found that the stochastic process for durables purchases is close to a random walk, a finding that implies that the quarterly deterioration rate for durables is about 100%. Although he did not pursue the idea, he noted that it appears that a model with adjustment costs would also be rejected by the data.

Bernanke (1984) examined purchases of automobiles within a 4-year panel of households. He assumes that households choose an optimal stock of autos through the standard rational expectations–permanent income model and then purchase autos at a rate given by a partial adjustment process. He did not try to justify the partial adjustment assumption through consideration of optimization, although a model of adjustment costs probably could yield his model as the outcome of optimization. The estimation method is similar to the one used by Hall and Mishkin (1982). His empirical findings reveal an adjustment rate of about 70% per year. His most interesting finding is that there is no evidence of excess sensitivity of auto purchases to transitory income. It appears that partial adjustment of consumption to current income is a competing explanation of facts that lead other investigators to conclude that liquidity constraints are important.

Bernanke (1985) developed a complete model with adjustment costs. Using quarterly U.S. data for durables, nondurables, and income, he found substantial excess sensitivity of both durables and nondurables within a model that posits constant real interest rates.

Mankiw (1985) studied durables in a framework that considers substitution between durables and nondurables and also intertemporal substitution. He found evidence of high elasticities of substitution in both dimensions. As a result, movements of real interest rates are an important influence making durables purchases depart from the predictions of a model that assumes constant real interest rates. He was unable to reject the hypothesis that income and consumption have the relation predicted by the simple rational expectations–permanent income model.

Bar-Ilan and Blinder (1987) developed a theory of durables purchases that takes explicit account of the lumpiness of durables. They showed that individual households will determine a range for the stock of each type of durable and make purchases or sell existing durables if the stock falls outside the range. They tackled the difficult problem of developing implications of the model for aggregate data, with somewhat mixed results.

7.1.7   Intertemporal Substitution

The effect of changes in interest rates on consumption and saving has always been an important topic of research on consumption. With the exception of Boskin (1978), there has been relatively little research on the traditional question of the role of the interest rate in the consumption function. The answer to that question is complicated because changes in the interest rate have both an income and a substitution effect. By contrast, the Euler equation formulation that has dominated research since the rational expectations revolution provides a way to measure the pure substitution effect of changes in interest rates.

The Euler equation for consumption with a variable real interest rate first appeared in the finance literature. Rubinstein (1976) contributed most of the basic model. The marriage of a constant-elasticity utility function with log-normally distributed returns provides a first-order condition in a highly tractable form. Breeden (1977, 1979) developed the intertemporal consumption model in the form that has been employed by countless authors in the past decade. The basic relation derived by Breeden can be written as

$$\Delta \log c_t = \frac{1}{\alpha} r_t + k + \varepsilon_t.$$

Here α is the coefficient of relative risk aversion, r_t is the mean of the distribution of the log of the value in $t + 1$ of a unit investment made at t, ε_t is a normally distributed disturbance, and k is a constant related to the covariance of r_t and $\Delta \log c_t$, to the variances of both variables, and to the rate of time preference. Breeden and his successors in the finance literature (Grossman and Shiller, 1982a,b; Shiller, 1982; Ferson, 1980; Breeden, 1983; and many others, many cited in the last reference) considered this equation to be part of a system with one equation for each type of investment. They defined the consumption beta of an investment as a normalization of the convariance of its return with the change in the log of consumption. Most of the literature in finance in this area has been devoted to measuring consumption betas and testing the relations among the betas and the mean returns of different investments.

Witihin the macroeconomic literature on consumption, the finance paper that has had the greatest influence is that by Hansen and Singleton

(1983). They estimated both single equations and systems of equations for multiple investments, using monthly consumptions and returns data. Their estimates of the coefficient of relative risk aversion, α, span a range centered on unity. They also tested and rejected the restrictions among the constants and covariances, but this finding has been more relevant for finance than for consumption. Additional results along this line appeared in Eichenbaum, Hansen, and Singleton (1986).

Hansen and Singleton's framework has been adopted by Summers (1982), Mankiw, Rotemberg, and Summers (1985), and Bean (1986) with similar results. Browning (1986a) has reached a similar specification by a somewhat different route. However, these subsequent papers have interpreted the coefficient of the expected real interest rate, r_t, on the right-hand side of a consumption growth equation as dealing with the propensity of consumers to substitute intertemporally from one period to the next. That is, they think of the equation in the form

$$\Delta \log c_t = \sigma r_t + k + \varepsilon_t.$$

Here σ is the intertemporal elasticity of substitution. A 1% rise in the expected real interest rate, r_t, causes the consumer to substitute σ percent of consumption from this year to the next. Formally, the difference is just the replacement of the reciprocal of the coefficient of relative risk aversion, $1/\alpha$, by σ, but a large difference of interpretation goes with that change.

Hall (1988) considered the question of the relation between these interpretations. The model underlying both the finance research and the macroeconomic research is founded upon an intertemporally separable utility function,

$$\sum e^{-\delta t} c_t^{1-\alpha}.$$

The parameter α controls the curvature of the one-period utility function and hence controls both the degree of risk aversion (the higher α is, the less willing the consumer is to substitute consumption among states of the world) and the degree of intertemporal substitution (the higher α is, the less willing the consumer is to substitute consumption among time periods). It is known that additive separability of the utility function together with the maximization of expected utility means that risky aversion and intertemporal substitution are controlled together by the curvature of the one-period utility function (Selden 1978).

Hall argued that the coefficient in an equation with the growth of consumption on the left and the expected real return from a particular investment on the right is the intertemporal elasticity of substitution, not the reciprocal of the coefficient of relative risk aversion. Risk aversion can be estimated using a system of two or more equations with investment of different riskiness, in which case the coefficient of relative risk aversion can be measured from the differences in the constants (as in Grossman and Shiller 1982a).

Hall's argument on this point is not conclusive, because there does not seem to be a convenient class of utility functions in which the two parameters are cleanly separated, except in the special case of only two periods. For the special case, Selden's results show that it is unambiguously the elasticity of intertemporal substitution and not the reciprocal of the coefficient of relative risk aversion that appears as the coefficient of the expected real interest rate in the consumption growth equation.

Viewed in this light, the previous research has found intertemporal elasticities of around one. Fluctuations in expected interest rates are a prime source of movements in consumption, according to the results. However, Hall questioned the finding of a substantial elasticity. Through the use of additional data for the interwar period and for the 1980s, when fluctuations in expected real rates were larger, and through a choice of instrumental variables that considers the timing of the data, he found values of the intertemporal elasticity close to zero, with reasonably small standard errors.

Muellbauer and Bover (1986) suggested a possible source of a downward bias in estimates of the intertemporal elasticity of substitution. They pointed out that aggregation may induce a negative correlation between the constant in the consumption growth equation and the interest rate— higher interest rates shift consumption toward groups, such as the elderly, with lower values of the constant.

Browning (1986c) took a very different approach to intertemporal substitution. He adapted nonparametric techniques developed by Varian to test the hypothesis that the observed sequence of consumption and interest rates are consistent with consumer choice under certainly. Under Browning's null hypothesis, all variations in consumption are attributed to intertemporal substitution and none to income surprises. He rejects the hypothesis for Canadian, U.K., and U.S. data, but there are extended subperiods when the hypothesis cannot be rejected.

7.1.8   Transitory Consumption and Shifts in Preferences

Flavin (1981), Hall and Mishkin (1982), and numerous other authors have noted that consumption may have a stochastic component not explained by the permanent income hypothesis. In panel data, the evidence for such a component is overwhelming; the component accounts for more of the variation of the first difference of consumption than does the component associated with changes in permanent income. Furthermore, in panel data, there is a presumption that at least part of the component is truly transitory consumption, because it arises from measuring consumption over a fairly brief period, so that changes in household inventories and the lumpiness of many purchases influences measured consumption.

In time-series data, where a general equilibrium analysis is mandatory, the diagnosis and treatment of transitory consumption is a much more difficult issue. Garber and King (1984) pointed out just how strong are the identifying assumptions needed to validate Euler-equation models in time-series data. In effect, either shifts in preference or other sources of changes in consumption other than changes in income or wealth must be assumed away, or special and questionable assumptions must be made about their stochastic properties. The easiest assumption, although very special, is that shifts in preferences occur as a random walk, so that the corresponding stochastic component in the first difference of consumption is unpredictable. Then the Euler equation has an extra stochastic term that satisfies the assumptions already made about the term that comes from the innovation in income or wealth. MaCurdy (1987) has set up a framework for studying consumption and labor supply in the presence of stochastic shifts of a very general type.

If shifts in preferences are anything but a random walk, then the Euler equation is probably not identified. Certainly the methods generally used for estimating the Euler equations are no longer valid. If shifts in preferences are stationary, although possibly serially correlated, then the first difference of consumption will have a component that is negatively serially correlated. The disturbance in period t will include the innovation in preferences in period $t - 1$ and possibly earlier as well. Because the earlier innovation shifted consumption, and a shift in consumption feeds back into income, variables dated $t - 1$ are no longer uncorrelated with the disturbance. In simple regression tests of the Euler equation with a fixed real interest rate, lagged income is no longer an appropriate regressor. The finding of significant coefficients for lagged income is no longer evidence against the rational expectations permanent income model. In more elaborate tests with variable expected real returns, lagged income is no longer eligible as an instrumental variable.

Hall (1986) attacked this problem by using an instrument that he considers truly exogenous: military spending. His objective was to isolate shifts in consumption associated with preference shifts from those associated with changes in well-being. He reasoned that changes in well-being cause movements along an expansion path for consumption of goods and leisure. The slope of the expansion path is revealed by the changes in the two variables brought about by changes in military spending. Then random shifts in preferences cause the two variables to depart from the expansion path. In other words, the residuals in the estimated consumption–work effort relation are a measure of the stochastic component of consumption associated with preference shifts. He found that the residuals are a dominant source of fluctuations in consumption itself and account for an important but not dominant fraction of fluctuations in total GNP. The only support in the work for the Euler equation approach is that the random shifts are at least approximately a random walk.

7.2 Conclusions

It is reasonably well established that the simple conclusion from the rational expectations–permanent income model with constant expected real interest rate is inconsistent with the data: The rate of change of consumption can be predicted by past values of real income and past values of a number of financial variables. Much of the recent literature on the macroeconomics of consumption can be seen as attempts to explain this finding.

Durable goods and the durability of consumption seem to explain the finding reasonably well. Hayashi's model with durable consumption leaves only a small role for liquidity constraints, and Mankiw's and Bernanke's models with durable goods accept the hypothesis of no explanatory power from lagged income.

Liquidity constraints can also explain the finding in a reasonably convincing way. Not only is the predictive power of income rationalized by only a modest incidence of liquidity constraints, but ancillary tests give reasonable results as well—for example, the predictive power of lagged income is concentrated among households with few liquid assets, according to Runkle and Zeldes, and unemployment displaces income as a predictor, according to Flavin. However, a model combining liquidity constraints and durable goods assigns all of the explanation for the predictive power of lagged income to durability and none to liquidity constraints, according to Bernanke.

Intertemporal substitution does not seem to be an important part of the explanation of the predictive power of lagged income and other variables. There is controversy about whether or not the intertemporal elasticity of substitution is large enough to make changes in expected interest rates an important factor in fluctuations in consumption growth. Nevertheless, no author has been able to show that predictive power of other variables disappears when intertemporal substitution is considered.

Acknowledgments

I am grateful to David Bizer for outstanding assistance. This research was supported by the National Science Foundation and is part of the NBER's program on economic fluctuations.

References

Altonji, J., and Aloysius Siow. 1987. Testing the Response of Consumption to Income Changes with (Noisy) Panel Data. *Quarterly Journal of Economics* 102: 293–328.

Ando, A., and F. Modigliani. 1963. The Life-Cycle Hypothesis of Saving: Aggregate Implications and Tests. *American Economic Review* 53: 55–84.

Bar-Ilan, A., and A. S. Blinder. 1987. The Life-Cycle Permanent-Income Model and Consumer Durables. Working paper 2149, National Bureau of Economic Research.

Bean, C. 1986. The Estimation of 'Surprise' Models and the 'Surprise' Consumption Function. *Review of Economic Studies* 53: 497–516.

Bernanke, B. S. 1984. Permanent Income, Liquidity, and Expenditure on Automobiles: Evidence from Panel Data. *Quarterly Journal of Economics* 99(3): 587–614.

Bernanke, B. S. 1985. Adjustment Costs, Durables, and Aggregate Consumption. *Journal of Monetary Economics* 15 (January): 41–68.

Berheim, B. D. 1987. Ricardian Equivalence: An Evaluation of Theory and Evidence. In S. Fischer (ed.), *NBER Macroeconomics Annual 1987*. Cambridge, Massachusetts: MIT Press, pp. 263–304.

Boskin, M. J. 1978. Taxation, Saving, and the Rate of Interest. *Journal of Political Economy* 86(2): S3–S27.

Breeden, D. T. 1977. Changing Consumption and Investment Opportunities and the Valuation of Securities. Unpublished doctoral dissertation, Stanford Graduate School of Business.

Breeden, D. T. 1979. An Intertemporal Asset Pricing Model with Stochastic Consumption and Investment Opportunities. *Journal of Financial Economics* 7: 265–296.

Breeden, D. T. 1983. Consumption, Production and Interest Rates: A Synthesis. Unpublished paper, Stanford University.

Browning, M. 1986a. The Intertemporal Allocation of Expenditure of Non-Durables, Services, and Durables. Unpublished paper, McMaster University.

Browning, M. 1986b. Testing Intertemporal Separability in Models of Households Behaviour. Unpublished paper, McMaster University.

Browning, M. 1986c. A Non-Parametric Test of the Life-Cycle Rational Expectations Hypothesis. Unpublished paper, McMaster University.

Browning, M. 1987. Eating, Drinking, Smoking, and Testing the Life-Cycle Hypothesis. *Quarterly Journal of Economics* 102: 329–345.

Campbell, J. Y. 1986. Does Saving Anticipate Declining Labor Income? An Alternative Test of the Permanent Income Hypothesis. Unpublished paper, Princeton University.

Campbell, J. Y., and R. H. Clarida. 1986. Household Saving and Permanent Income in Canada and the United Kingdom. Unpublished paper.

Campbell, J. Y., and A. Deaton. 1987. Is Consumption Too Smooth? Working paper 2134, National Bureau of Economic Research.

Chang, F.-R. 1987. A Theory of the Consumption Function with Wages Fluctuations. Unpublished paper, Indiana University.

Christiano, L. J. 1984. The Effects of Aggregation over Time on Tests of the Representative Agent Model of Consumption. Unpublished paper, University of Chicago and Carnegie Mellon University.

Christiano, L. J. 1987. Is Consumption Insufficiently Sensitive to Innovations in Income? Working paper 333, Research Department, Federal Reserve Bank of Minneapolis.

Christiano, L. J., M. Eichenbaum, and D. Marshall. 1987. The Permanent Income Hypothesis Revisited. Working paper 335, Research Department, Federal Reserve Bank of Minneapolis.

Cuddington, J. T. 1982. Canadian Evidence on the Permanent Income–Rational Expectations Hypothesis. *Canadian Journal of Economics* 15(2): 331–335.

Cuddington, J. T., and Hurd, M. D. 1981. Valid Statistical Tests of the Permanent Income–Rational Expectations Hypothesis. Unpublished paper.

Daly, V., and Hadjimatheous, G. 1981. Stochastic Implications of the Life-Cycle–Permanent Income Hypothesis: Evidence for the U.K. Economy. *Journal of Political Economy* 98(3): 596–599.

Darby, M. R. 1972. The Allocation of Transitory Income among Consumers' Assets. *American Economic Review* 64(4): 928–941.

Deaton, A. 1986. Life-Cycle Models of Consumption: Is the Evidence Consistent with the Theory? Working paper 1910, National Bureau of Economic Research.

Eichenbaum, M. S., L. P. Hansen, and K. J. Singleton. 1986. A Time Series Analysis of Representative Agent Models of Consumption and Leisure Choice under Uncertainty. Working paper 1981, National Bureau of Economic Research.

Evans, O. 1982. The Life Cycle Inheritance: Theoretical and Empirical Essays on the Life Cycle Hypothesis of Saving. Unpublished doctoral dissertation, University of Pennsylvania.

Ferson, W. 1980. Consumption, Inflation, and the Term Structure of Interest Rates. Unpublished paper.

Ferson, W. E., and J. J. Merrick, Jr. Forthcoming. Nonstationarity and Stage-of-the-Business-Cycle Effects in Consumption-Based Asset Pricing Relations. *Journal of Financial Economics.*

Flavin, M. A. 1981. The Adjustment of Consumption to Changing Expectations about Future Income. *Journal of Political Economy* 98(5): 1020–1037.

Flavin, M. A. 1985. Excess Sensitivity of Consumption to Current Income: Liquidity Constraints or Myopia? *Canadian Journal of Economics* 18 (February): 117–136.

Friedman, M. 1986. The Role of Monetary Policy. *American Economics Review* 58: 1–17.

Garber, P., and R. King. 1984. Deep Structural Excavation? A Critique of Euler Equation Methods. Presented at NBER Research Program on Economic Fluctuations Macro Conference.

Goodfriend, M. 1986. Information-Aggregation Bias: The Case of Consumption. Unpublished paper, Federal Reserve Bank of Richmond and University of Rochester.

Grossman, S. J., A Melino, and R. J. Shiller. 1985. Estimating the Continuous Time Consumption Based Asset Pricing Model. Working paper 1643, National Bureau of Economic Research.

Grossman, S. J., and R. J. Shiller. 1982a. The Determinants of the Variability of Stock Market Prices. *American Economic Review* 71(2): 222–227.

Grossman, S. J., and R. J. Shiller. 1982b. Consumption Correlatedness and Risk Measurement in Economies with Non-Traded Assets, and Heterogeneous Information. *Journal of Financial Economics* 10(2): 195–210.

Hall, R. E. 1978. Stochastic Implications of the Life Cycle-Permanent Income Hypothesis: Theory and Evidence. *Journal of Political Economy* 86(6): 971–987.

Hall, R. E. 1986. The Role of Consumption in Economic Fluctuations. In R. J. Gordon (ed.), *The American Business Cycle: Continuity and Change.* Chicago: The University of Chicago Press, 237–255.

Hall, R. E. 1988. Intertemporal Substitution Consumption, *Journal of Political Economy* 96: 339–357.

Hall, R. E., and F. S. Mishkin. 1982. The Sensitivity of Consumption to Transitory Income: Estimates from Panel Data on Households. *Econometrica* 50(2): 461–481.

Hansen, L. P., S. F. Richard, and K. J. Singleton. 1981. Econometric Implications of the Intertemporal Capital Asset Pricing Model. Unpublished paper, Carnegie Mellon University.

Hansen, L. P., and K. J. Singleton. 1983. Stochastic Consumption, Risk Aversion, and the Temporal Behavior of Stock Market Returns. *Journal of Political Economy* 91(2): 249–365.

Hansen, L. P., and K. J. Singleton. 1986. Efficient Estimation of Linear Asset Pricing Models with Moving Average Errors. Unpublished paper, University of Chicago, Harvard University, and Carnegie Mellon University.

Hayashi, F. 1985. The Permanent Income Hypothesis and Consumption Durability: Analysis Based on Japanese Panel Data. *Quarterly Journal of Economics* 100 (November): 1083–113.

Hayashi, F. 1987. Tests for Liquidity Constraints: A Critical Survey and Some New Observations. In T. Bewley (ed.), *Advances in Econometrics, Fifth World Congress,* vol. 2. Cambridge: Cambridge University Press, pp. 91–120.

Jacobson, R. 1981. Testing the Implications of the Life Cycle–Permanent Income Hypothesis. Unpublished paper, University of California, Berkeley.

Johnson, P. 1983. Life-Cycle Consumption under Rational Expectations: Some Australian Evidence. *Economic Record* 59: 345–350.

Kormendi, R. C., and L. LaHaye. 1986. Cross-Regime Tests of the Permanent Income Hypothesis. Working paper, University of Michigan.

Lucas, R. E. 1976. Econometric Policy Evaluation: A Critique. In K. Brunner and A. H. Meltzer (eds.), *Carnegie-Rochester Series on Public Policy*, vol. 1. Amsterdam: North-Holland.

MaCurdy, T. E. 1987. Modeling the Time Series Implications of Life-cycle Theory. Unpublished paper, Stanford University.

Mankiw, G. N. 1982. Hall's Consumption Hypothesis and Durable Goods. *Journal of Monetary Economics* 10(3): 417–425.

Mankiw, G. N. 1985. Consumer Durables and the Real Interest Rate. *The Review of Economics and Statistics* 67(3): 353–362.

Mankiw, G. N., J. Rotemberg, and L. Summers. 1985. Intertemporal Substitution in Macroeconomics. *Quarterly Journal of Economics* 100(1): 225–251.

Mankiw, G. N., and M. D. Shapiro, 1985a. Risk and Return: Consumption Beta Versus Market Beta. Discussion Paper No. 738, Cowles Foundation.

Mankiw, G. N., and M. D. Shapiro, 1985b. Trends, Random Walks, and Tests of the Permanent Income Hypothesis. *Journal of Monetary Economics* 16(2): 165–174.

Marsh, T. A. 1984. On Euler-Equation Restrictions on the Temporal Behavior of Asset Returns. Working paper 1619–84, Alfred P. Sloan School of Management.

Miron, J. A. 1986. Seasonal Fluctuations and the Life Cycle–Permanent Income Model of Consumption. *Journal of Political Economy* 94 (December): 1258–1279.

Mork, K. A., and V. K. Smith. 1986. Another Test of the Life-Cycle Hypothesis, but with Much Improved Panel Data. Unpublished paper, Vanderbilt University.

Muellbauer, J. 1983. Surprises in the Consumption Function. *Economic Journal* 93(suppl.): 34–40.

Muellbauer, J., and O. Bover. 1986. Liquidity Constraints and Aggregation in the Consumption Function under Uncertainty. Discussion paper 12, Oxford Institute of Economics and Statistics.

Muth, J. 1960. Optimal Properties of Exponentially Weighted Forecasts. *Journal of the American Statistical Association* 55: 299–306.

Nelson, C. R. 1987. A Reappraisal of Recent Tests of the Permanent Income Hypothesis. *Journal of Political Economy* 95: 641–646.

Rubinstein, M. 1976. The Strong Case for the Generalized Logarithmic Utility Model as the Premier Model of Financial Markets. *The Journal of Finance* 31(2): 551–571.

Runkle, D. 1983. Liquidity Constraints and the Permanent Income Hypothesis: Evidence from Panel Data. Unpublished paper, Brown University.

Sargent, T. J. 1978. Rational Expectations, Econometric Exogeneity, and Consumption. *Journal of Political Economy* 86(4): 673–700.

Sargent, T. J., and L. P. Hansen. 1981. Formulation and Estimating Dynamic Linear Rational Expectations Models. In R. Lucas and T. Sargent (eds.), *Rational Expectations and Econometric Practice*, vol. 1. Minneapolis: University of Minneapolis Press, pp. 91–125.

Selden, L. 1978. A New Representation of Preferences over 'Certain X Uncertain' Consumption Pairs: The 'Ordinal Certainty Equivalent' Hypothesis. *Econometrica* 46 (September): 1045–1060.

Shiller, R. J. Consumption, Asset Markets, and Macroeconomic Fluctuations. *Carnegie-Rochester Conference Series on Public Policy* 17 (Autumn): 203–238.

Sims, C., J. H. Stock, and M. W. Watson. 1987. Inference in Linear Time Series Models with Some Unit Roots. Hoover Working Papers in Economics E-87-1, Hoover Institution.

Stock, J. H., and K. D. West. 1987. Integrated Regressors and Tests of the Permanent Income Hypothesis. Unpublished paper, Harvard University, Princeton University, Stanford University, and the NBER.

Summers, L. 1982. Tax Policy, the Rate of Return, and Savings. Working paper 995, National Bureau of Economic Research.

West, K. D. 1986. The Insensitivity of Consumption to News about Income. Unpublished paper. Princeton University.

Working, H. 1960. Note on the Correlation of First Differences of Averages in a Random Chain. *Econometrica* 28: 916–918.

Zeldes, S. 1985. Consumption and Liquidity Constraints: An Empirical Investigation. Paper 24-85, Rodney L. White Center for Financial Research.

Zeldes, S. 1986. Optimal Consumption with Stochastic Income: Deviations from Certainty Equivalence. Unpublished paper, University of Pennsylvania.

8 The Role of Consumption in Economic Fluctuations

8.1 The Issues

Consumption is the dominant component of GNP. A 1% change in consumption is five times the size of a 1% change in investment. This chapter investigates whether the behavior of consumers is an independent source of macroeconomic fluctuations or whether most disturbances come from other sectors.

Informal commentaries on the business cycle put considerable weight on the independent behavior of consumption. It is commonplace to hear of a business revival sparked by consumers. On the other hand, all modern theories of fluctuations make the consumer a reactor to economic events, not a cause of them. Random shocks in technology are generally the driving force in fully articulated models.

This chapter develops a framework where the distinction between a movement along a consumption schedule and shift of the schedule is well defined. Application of the framework to twentieth-century American data shows that shifts of the consumption schedule have probably been an important case of fluctuations but have probably not been the dominant source of them.

I consider three sources of disturbances to the economy: (1) shifts of the consumption schedule; (2) shifts of the schedule relating spending in categories other than consumption and miliary spending; and (3) shifts in military spending. The reason for the explicit examination of military spending is that such spending is the only plainly exogenous major influence on the economy. Movements in military spending reveal the slopes of the consumption schedule and other spending schedules.

My basic strategy is the following. Fluctuations in military spending reveal the slope of the consumption/GNP schedule. GNP rises with military spending—quite stably, GNP has risen by about 62 cents for every dollar increase in military spending. This conclusion is supported by data from years other than those of major wars, when resource allocation by command may have made the consumption schedule irrelevant. But when GNP rises under the stimulus of increased military spending, consumption

Reprinted with permission from "The Role of Consumption in Economic Fluctuations," in Robert J. Gorden (ed.), *The American Business Cycle: Continuity and Change*, National Bureau of Economic Research Conference on Business Cycles (Chicago: University of Chicago Press, 1986), pp. 237–255.

actually falls a little—the same dollar of military spending has depressed consumption by about 7 cents.

Under the reasonable assumption that higher military spending does not shift the consumption schedule but only moves consumers along the schedule, we can infer the slope of the schedule from the ratio of the consumption change to the GNP change. The slope is essentially zero.

Equipped with this knowledge, we can measure the shift of the consumption schedule as the departure of consumption from a schedule with the estimated slope. My main concern is the absolute and relative importance of these shifts.

The effect of a consumption shift on GNP depends on the slope of the consumption schedule and also upon the slope of the schedule relating other spending to GNP. For this reason it is necessary to carry out a similar exercise for other spending. Again, the way other spending changes when military spending absorbs added resources is the way the slope can be inferred. Historically, other spending has declined when military spending has risen; investment, net exports, and nonmilitary government purchases are crowded out by military spending. For each dollar of added military spending, other spending declines by about 30 cents. The inference is that the schedule relating other spending to GNP has an important negative slope.

Over the period studied here, the correlation of the change in consumption and the change in GNP has been strong; the correlation coefficient is 0.59. Similarly, the correlation of the change in other spending and the change in GNP is strongly positive at 0.61. The results of this paper explain *all* of the correlation of consumption and GNP in terms of the unexplained shifts in the two schedules and *none* as the result of movements along the consumption function. Even more strikingly, the results explain the strong *positive* correlation of other spending and GNP in spite of the *negative* slope of the schedule relating the two.

Stated in terms of the scale of the economy in 1982, the standard deviation of the annual first difference of GNP for the period was $90 billion. The standard deviation of the component associated with the shift of the consumption function was $28 billion; for other spending including military, $72 billion. The decomposition between the two schedule shifts is ambiguous because they are highly correlated, but by assumption both are uncorrelated with the shift in military spending.

Because the slightly negative slope found for the consumption function in this work contradicts the thinking of many macroeconomists on this subject, I have repeated the exercise for two assumed values for the slope of the consumption/GNP schedule. One, which I think of as Keynesian, assumes a value of 0.3. The standard deviation of the consumption shift effect on GNP is $26 billion. The shifts in the consumption function are estimated to be smaller in this case, but their contribution to movements in GNP is larger because the multiplier is larger.

A second case derives from equilibrium models of the business cycle. It interprets the consumption/GNP schedule as the expansion path of the consumption/labor supply decision of the household. The slope of the schedule should be *negative*, since presumably both consumption and leisure are normal goods. Any events that make people feel it is a good idea to consume more should also cause them to take more leisure and therefore work less. A reasonable value for the slope of the consumption/GNP schedule under this interpretation is -1. When this is imposed on the problem, the consumption shifts appear much larger, since this is a long step away from the regression relation. The standard deviation of the effect of consumption on GNP is $47 billion, comparable to the effect of shifts in other spending. $46 billion.

8.2 Earlier Research

Modern thinking about the possible role of shifts in the consumption function in overall macro fluctuations began with Milton Friedman and Gary Becker's "A Statistical Illusion in Judging Keynesian Models" (1957). They pointed out that random shifts in the consumption function could induce a positive correlation between consumption and income, which in turn could make the consumption look more responsive to income than it really was and also make the consumption function more reliable than it really was. However, neither Friedman and Becker nor other workers on the consumption function pursued the idea that shifts in the consumption function might be an important element of the business cycle.

More recently, Peter Temin's *Did Monetary Forces Cause the Great Depression?* (1976) argued forcefully for a role for shifts of the consumption function in explaining the contraction from 1929 to 1933. Temin focuses particularly on the residual from a consumption function in the year 1930 and suggests that the shift in consumption in that year was an important factor in setting off the contraction. His results are strongly supported in this paper, which finds large shifts in the consumption/GNP relation in all the years of the contraction.

Temin's critics, Thomas Mayer (1980) and Barry Anderson and James Butkiewicz (1980), confirm that consumption functions of various types had important negative residuals in 1930. It is a curious feature of Temin's work and that of his critics that no attention has been paid to the issue of finding the true slope of the consumption/income schedule. If the history of the United States is full of episodes where consumption shifts affected GNP, then the observed correlation of consumption and income is no guide at all to the slope of the consumption function. Temin considerably under-states the power of his case by looking for departures from the historical relation between consumption and income, which is not at all the same thing as the slope of the structural relation. The historical relation sum-marizes numerous other episodes where a spontaneous shift in consump-tion had important macro effects. Temin looks only at the excess in 1930 over the usual amount of a shift, when his argument logically involves the whole amount of the shift.

Because of my use of military spending as the exogenous instrument that identifies the structural consumption function, I spend some effort here in understanding how a burst of military purchases influences the economy. Robert Barro (1981) has examined the theory of the effect of government purchases in an equilibrium framework and has studied United States data on the effect on GNP. He found a robust positive effect of all types of government purchases, with an especially large coefficient for temporary military spending. My results here are in line with Barro's, though I do not attempt to distinguish permanent and temporary purchases. Barro notes that higher government purchases should *depress* consumption as a matter of theory (p. 1094) but does not examine the actual behavior of consump-tion. Barro and Robert King (1982) point out he difficulties of creating a theoretical equilibrium model in which the covariance of consumption and work effort is anything but sharply negative.

Joseph Altonji (1982) and N. Gregory Mankiw, Julio Rotemberg, and Lawrence Summers (1982) use the observed positive covariation of con-sumption and hours of work to cast doubt on the empirical validity of equilibrium models. However, neither paper considers the possibility that feedback from shifts in household behavior creates an econometric identification problem. The results of this paper give partial support to their conclusion. With a serious treatment of the identification problem, the structural relation between work and consumption appears to be flat or slightly negatively sloped, but not nearly enough negatively sloped to fit the predictions of the equilibrium model.

Here I examine the importance of fluctuations in consumption as an interesting question in its own right. My finding of important shifts in the consumption function is also important for recent research on consumption and related issues in finance. As Peter Garber and Robert King (1983) point out, shifts in preferences or other sources of unexplained fluctuations in consumption behavior invalidate the Euler equation approach I and others have used in studying the reaction of consumers to surprises in income and to changes in expected real interest rates. The hope that the Euler equation is identified econometrically without the use of exogenous variables depends critically on the absence of the type of shift found in this paper. My findings suggest that the Euler equation is identified only through the use of exogenous instruments, just as are most other macro-economic structural relations.

8.3 A Simple Structural Relation between GNP and Consumption

Keynesian theory denies consumers choice about the level of work effort. The effective demand process dictates the amount of work and the corresponding level of earnings. Consumers choose consumption so as to maximize satisfaction given actual and expected earnings. In general, the resulting relationship between earnings and cconsumption can be complicated—consumers will use the information contained in current and lagged earnings to infer likely future earnings and thus the appropriate level of consumption. Traditional Keynesian though has emphasized the strength of the contemporaneous relation between income and comsumption. Liquidity constraints probably contribute to the strength. Recent tests by Hall and Mishkin (1982) and by Marjorie Flavin (1981) have rejected the optimal response of consumption in favor of excess sensitivity to current income (however, these tests are likely to be contaminated by shifts in consumer behavior of the type investigated in this paper).

Otto Eckstein and Allen Sinai's paper in this volume (chapter 1) provides a reasonable estimate for the slope of the GNP/consumption schedule in a Keynesian framework. In their table 1.7, they estimate the effects on GNP and consumption of an exogenous increase in government purchases. The ratio of the change in consumption to the change in GNP is an estimate of the slope of exactly the schedule considered in this paper. The ratio is as follows.

Quarters after increase	GNP	Consumption	Ratio
4	1.26	0.41	0.32
8	0.94	0.28	0.30
12	0.81	0.18	0.22
16	0.64	0.10	0.16
24	0.56	0.10	0.18

I will use an estimate for the year-to-year marginal propensity to consume of 0.3 on the basis of this evidence about the overall behavior of a fully developed Keynesian model.

8.3.1 Equilibrium Thinking about the Consumption/GNP Schedule

In an equilibrium model consumers are free to choose the most satisfying combination of hours of work and consumption of goods, subject to the market trade-off between the two (see figure 8.1):

$$\max_{\{c_t, y_t\}} \Sigma D^t u(c_t, y_t)$$

subject ot $\Sigma R_t(p_t c_t - w_t y_t) = W.$

My notation is as follows:

D = time preference factor;

$u(\ )$ = one-year utility function;

c_t = consumption in year t;

y_t = employment in year t;

R_t = discount factor;

p_t = price of consumption goods in year t;

w_t = wage in year t;

W = initial wealth.

CONSUMPTION

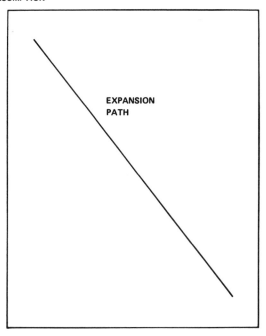

WORK

Figure 8.1
The expansion path. For a given real wage, consumption and work occur in combinations given by the path. The real interest rate and the level of wealth determine the position on the expansion path chosen by the consumer.

I will work with one aspect of the overall problem, the consumption/work choice in year t. The first-order condition for that choice is

marginal rate of substitution = real wage

or

$$-\frac{\partial u/\partial y_t}{\partial u/\partial c_t} = \frac{w_t}{p_t} = \omega_t$$

Define the expansion path, $f(y_t, \omega_t)$, by

$$-\frac{\partial u(f(y,\omega), y)/\partial y}{\partial u(f(y,\omega), y)/\partial c} = \omega.$$

Other aspects of the overall choice problem determine the point the consumer chooses on the expansion path. These include wealth and the timing of consumption and work. With the real wage held constant, higher wealth moves the consumer to a point of higher consumption and lower work. Again with the real wage held constant, a higher real interest rate moves the consumer to a point of lower consumption and more work. Altonji (1982) pointed out the usefulness of examining the joint behavior of work effort, consumption, and the real wage; his paper presents many more details on the derivation of their relationship.

It should be apparent that the expansion path slopes downward as long as consumption and leisure are normal goods.

The expansion path shifts downward if the real wage declines. Consequently, a higher tax rate depresses consumption given the level of work effort. On the other hand, the expansion path is unaffected by an increase in government purchases of goods and services or by lump-sum transfers or taxes. These latter influences will move the consumer along the expansion path but will not shift the path.

The slope of the expansion path can be estimated as the negative of the ratio of the income effect in the demand for consumption goods to the income effect in the labor supply function. Estimated income effects for labor supply run on the order of 50 cents less in earnings for each dollar in increased nonlabor income. That is, an increase in nonlabor income of $1 raises toal income by only 50 cents. If all of the increase in total income sooner or later is applied to goods consumption, then the income effect for goods consumption is also 50 cents per dollar of nonlabor income. The resulting slope of the expansion path is -1.

The structural relation in the equilibrium model refers to consumption and work effort. For the purposes of this paper, I think the best measure of the change in work effort from one year to the next is the change in real GNP. In the short run, the amount of capital available for use in production hardly changes, though of course the intensity of its use changes. Almost all changes in output correspond to changes in hours of labor input and in the amount of effort per hour spent on the job (see Hall 1980 for an elaboration and empirical study of this point). Real GNP is the best available measure of all the dimensions of changes in work effort in the short run.

The structural relation suggested by the equilibrium model has the form

$$c_t = \beta y_t + \gamma \omega_t.$$

In addition to the level of work effort, measured by y_t, the after-tax real wage, ω_t, shifts consumption up relative to work effort. In the empirical work carried out here, it is not possible to estimate the coefficients of two different endogenous variables. The best that can be done is to estimate the coefficient of y, net of the part of a real wage movement that is systematically related to y. For example, if the real wage is countercyclical, so that

$$\omega_t = -\delta y_t,$$

then it is possible to esimate the net relation,

$$c_t = (\beta - \gamma \delta) y_t.$$

Because β is negative, the countercyclical wage movements makes the consumption/GNP relation even more negatively sloped. It seems unlikely that procyclical movements of after-tax real wages are anywhere near large enough to explain my finding here of a zero net slope of the consumption/GNP relation. That finding is probably evidence against a pure equilibrium model.

8.3.2   Synthesis

Equilibrium and Keynesian models agree on a structural relation between consumption and income or work of the form

$$c_t = \beta y_t + \varepsilon_t.$$

Here,

β = slope of the structural relation, negative for the equilibrium model
(say -1), positive for the Keynesian model (say 0.3);

ε_t = random shift in the c-y relation.

8.4   Other Components of GNP

I will assume that military purchases of goods and services, g_t, is an exogenous variable.

I will define x_t as the remainder of GNP, that is, investment plus net exports plus nonmilitary government purchases of goods and services (the latter is largely state and local). x_t has a structural relation to GNP; fluctuations in this relation are a source of fluctuations in almost all theories of the business cycle.

It is not possible to estimate a detailed structural model for x_t for the reason just mentioned—a single exogenous variable limits estimation to a single endogenous variable. Basically, what can be estimated is the net effect of an increase in GNP on investment, net exports, and nonmilitary government purchases. On the one hand, considerations of the accelerator (particularly important for inventory investment) suggest a positive relation between GNP and x. On the other hand, increases in interest rates that accompany an increase in GNP bring decreases in x. For investment, especially in housing. the negative response to interest rates is well documented. For net exports, an increase in GNP raises imports directly. In addition, under floating exchange rates, the higher interest rates brought by higher GNP cause the dollar to appreciate, making imports cheaper to the United States and exports more expensive to the rest of the world. It is perfectly reasonable that the overall net effect of higher GNP on investment, net exports, and nonmilitary purchases should be negative.

The following simple relation summarizes these considerations:

$x_t = \mu y_t + v_t.$

The coefficient μ may well be negative, if crowding out through interest rates is an important phenomenon.

8.5 The Complete Model

The model comprises three equations:

$$c_t = \beta y_t + \varepsilon_t$$

$$x_t = \mu y_t + v_t$$

$$y_t = c_t + x_t + g_t.$$

The solutions for GNP is

$$y_t = \frac{1}{1 - \beta - \mu}(g_t + \varepsilon_t + v_t).$$

This equation gives a precise accounting for the sources of fluctuations in output. The three driving forces for the economy are military purchases of goods and serivces, g_t, the random shift in the consumption schedule, ε_t, and the random shift in other spending, v_t.

8.6 Identification and Estimation

The goals of estimation in this work are threefold:

1. Estimate the multiplier,

$$\frac{1}{1 - \beta - \mu},$$

which applies to each of the three components in the decomposition in the last section.

2. Estimate the "propensity to consume," β, in order to compute the residuals, ε_t, in the consumption function.

3. Estimate the "propensity to spend," μ, in the order to compute the residuals, v_t, in the function for other spending.

The solution to the first problem is perfectly straightforward. In the equation for the movement in GNP, military spending appears as a right-hand variable along with two disturbances assumed to be uncorrelated with military spending. Hence the regression of GNP on military spending should estimate the multiplier directly. Again, the interpretation of the estimated multiplier is net of feedback effects through interest rates.

To estimate the slope of the consumption/GNP schedule, β, note that c and g have the regression relation

$$c_t = \frac{\beta}{1 - \beta - \mu}(g_t + v_t) + \frac{1 - \mu}{1 - \beta - \mu}\varepsilon_t.$$

An estimate of β can be computed as the ratio of this coefficient to the multiplier. Alternatively, exactly the same estimate can be computed with two-stage least squares applied to the c-y relation with g as the instrument.

The slope of the x-y relation can be computed analogously either by the ratio of the regression coefficient of x on g to the multiplier or by applying two-stage least squares to the x-y equation with g as instrument.

The relationships estimated in this chapter are approximations to more complicated equations. For example, the complete model does not do justice to the modern Keynesian notion that gradual wage and price adjustment gives the model a tendency toward full employment in the long run. The results are likely to look somewhat different with an estimation technique that gives heavy weight to lower frequencies from those based more on higher frequencies. Because cyclical fluctuations are the focus here, I want to exclude the lower frequencies from the estimation. I have accomplished the exclusion in two ways. First, I have detrended all the data in a consistent fashion. Second, I have used first differences in all of the basic estimation. With annual data, using first differences puts strong weight on the cyclical frequencies and no weight at all on the lowest frequqencies.

8.7 Data

The data on real GNP in 1972 dollars for 1919–82 and real personal consumption expenditures for 1929–82 are from the United States national income and product accounts (NIPA). For 1919–28, data on real consumption were taken from John Kendrick (1961).

I used data on real military purchases of goods and serivces from the NIPA for 1972 through 1982 and from Kendrick for 1919–53. For 1954 through 1971, nominal military spending was taken from the NIPA and deflated by the implicit deflator for national security spending from the Office of Management and Budget (1983), converted to a calendar-year basis.

For some additional results described at the end of the chapter, I used the number of full-time equivalent employees in all industries, including military, from the NIPA.

To eliminate the noncyclical frequencies from the data, I started by fitting a trend to real GNP:

$$\log y_t = 5.14 + 0.0206\,t + 0.00014\,t^2.$$
(t is one in 1909)

Then I detrended real GNP, real consumption, and real military purchases with this real GNP trend. I preserved the 1982 values of each of the three variables, so the effect of detrending was to raise the earlier levels. For employment, I detrended with a log-linear trend of 1.96% per year and rebased the series so that it equals real GNP in 1982.

All of the estimates used the first differences of the detrended series.

8.8   Results

All of the regression reported here include intercepts, but the values of the intercepts are not reported because detrending makes them almost meaningless.

Estimation of the multiplier by regressing the chance in GNP on the change in military spending for the years 1920–40 and 1947–82 gives the following results:

$$\Delta y_t = .62\,\Delta g_t.$$
$$\quad\;(.16)$$

SE: $81 billion;   D-W: 1.48

Because the multiplier is less than one, it is clear that a certain amount of crowding out took place, on the average. Each dollar of military purchases raises GNP by 62 cents so nonmilitary uses of output decline by 38 cents.

The regression of consumption on military spending is

$$\Delta c_t = -0.07\,\Delta g_t$$
$$\quad\;(0.08)$$

SE: $38 billion;   D-W: 1.50

Because the coefficient is close to zero, with a small standard error, it is clear that the implied slope of the c-y relation will be close to zero as well. Even though periods of wartime controls on consumption have been omitted from this regression, there is strong evidence against the proposition that those increases in GNP that can be associated with exogenous increases in military spending stimulated any important increases in consumption. Similarly, the strong *negative* response of consumption to military spending predicted by the equilibrium model has also been shown to be absent.

The ratio of the two regression coefficients is -0.12; this is the estimate of the slope of the consumption/GNP schedule. The same estimate can be obtained by two-stage least squares, together with the standard error of β and the standard error of the residuals:

$$\Delta c_t = -0.12 \, \Delta y_t.$$
$$(0.15)$$

SE: $46 billion;   D-W: 1.39

The confidence interval on the slope of the c-y relation includes a range of values but excludes the Keynesian value of 0.3 and the equilibrium values of -1 as well. Neither theory is able to explain the lack of a structural association of consumption and GNP.

In the next section I will make use of consumption equations with two different assumed values of the slope:

Keynesian:

$\beta = 0.3$

$\Delta c_t = 0.3 \, \Delta y_t$

SE: $31 billion

Equilibrium:

$\beta = -1$

$\Delta c_t = -\Delta y_t$

SE: $117 billion.

The basic results of the paper can be guessed from these results. The residuals in the Keynesian consumption relation are smaller than those for the estimated relation (standard errors of $31 billion against $46 billion) and are very much smaller than are those for the equilibrium case ($117 billion). Even the smaller Keynesian residuals turn out to be important in the overall determination of GNP. GNP and consumption are positively

correlated both because the consumption relation slopes upward and because shifts in the relation are an important determinant of both variables.

On the other hand, the equilibrium model sees very large shifts in the
c-y relation. When the relation shifts upward, both c and y rise. Because
most of the variation in both variables comes from the shifts in the relation,
the two are highly positively correlated, even though the relation has a
negative slope. That a positive slope gives a better fit in the consumption
equation is not evidence against the equilibrium view at all.

8.8.1   Results for Other Spending, x

The regression of Δx on Δg gives

$$\Delta x_t = -0.30 \Delta g_t.$$
$$\quad\;\; (.12)$$

SE: $58 billion;   D-W: 2.03

Investment, net exports, and nonmilitary government spending are quite
strongly *negatively* influenced by military spending, again during years
when wartime controls on private spending were not in effect. The estimate
of the slope of the x-y schedule inferred by dividing by the multiplier is
-0.48. The same estimate is available from two-stage least squares:

$$\Delta x_t = -0.48 \Delta y_t.$$
$$\quad\;\; (0.30)$$

SE: $95 billion;   D-W: 1.79

Plainly, the negative effects operating through interest rates dominate the
positive effects of the accelerator. Higher GNP depresses nonconsumption,
nonmilitary spending along this structural schedule.

8.9   Estimates of the Importance of the Consumption Shift

Because neither of the major schools of business cycle theory is consistent
with my estimates of the slope of the c-y relaton, I will make estimates for
three different cases:

1.   Estimated.   The slope of the c-y relation is -0.12, the value inferred
from the fact that, historically, higher military purchases have raised GNP

but not conumption. Consumption is virtually an exogenous variable. It influences GNP but is not influenced by GNP.

2. Keynesian. The slope of of the c-y relation is 0.3. When more work is available, people consume more as well.

3. Equilibrium. The slope of the c-y relation is -1. Events that move consumers along their expansion paths leave the sum of GNP and consumption unchanged. Departures of the sum of GNP and consumption are a signal of a shift in the expansion path, possibly associated with a change in the after-tax real wage, but usually a random, unexplained shift.

Though the movements of GNP can be decomposed into three components for the three driving forces listed in the model in section 8.4 (military purchases, the random shift in the consumption schedule, and the random shift in the investment/exports schedule), I will concentrate on the consumption shift on the one hand and the sum of the two other components on the other hand. The consumption component is

$$\frac{1}{1 - \beta - \mu}\dot{\varepsilon}_t,$$

where ε_t is the residual from the consumption equation. Note that the magnitude of the consumption component depends on the magnitude of the residual and on the magnitude of the multiplier. The other component is just Δy_t less the consumption component.

Figure 8.2 shows the total change in real GNP and the consumption components for the three cases. As a general matter, the consumption component is most important for the equilibrium case and least important for the Keynesian case. However, it is a significant contributor to GNP fluctuations in all three cases.

Under the estimated results where consumption is effectively exogenous, shifts in the consumption schedule are important, but so are shifts in the other determinants of GNP, especially in the interwar period. Responsibility for the Great Contraction is shared between shifts in the c-y relation and the other sources. However, in the postwar period, shifts in other spending account for the bulk of the movement of GNP. The two large drops of GNP in 1973–74 and 1974–75 are partly the result of drops in conumption. Some of the long contraction since 1978 is the result of a consumption shift as well.

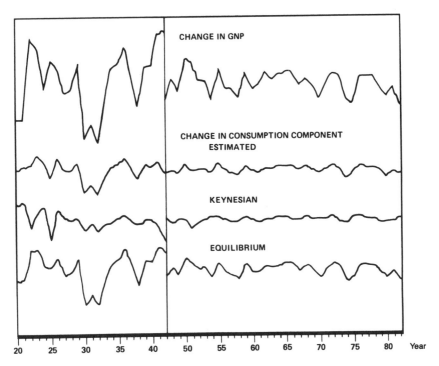

Figure 8.2
Change in real GNP and the consumption component for the three cases

In the Keynesian view, shifts in the consumption function are bound to be less important than in the other two cases. When consumption and GNP drop together, all or part of the decline in consumption can be attributed to the drop in GNP. Still, shifts in consumption are a part of the story of total fluctuations.

For the equilibrium case, the story about the Great Contraction in 1929–32 told by these results will help clarify what the theory is saying. Rescaled real GNP fell by $227 billion in 1929–30, $171 billion in 1930–31, and $243 billion in 1931–32. Of this, $140 billion came from a random shift in household behavior toward less work and less consumption in 1929–30, $97 billion in 1930–31, and $148 billion in 1931–32. The remaining $87 billion in the first year, $74 billion in the second year, and $95 billion in the third year came from changes in military spending and shifts in the investment/exports schedule. Of the two, the first was almost negligible.

Table 8.1
Statistical summary

Standard deviation of change	Keynesian	Case estimated	Equilibrium
Real GNP	90	93	93
Consumption component	26	28	47
Other component	97	72	46
Correlation of two components	−0.40	0.53	0.86

Note: Standard deviations are in billions of 1972 dollars, with quantities rescaled to 1982 magnitudes.

But the most important part of the story of the contraction was a sudden lack of interest in working consuming, according to the equilibrium model.

Table 8.1 summarizes the findings for the three cases in terms of simple statistical measures. It is interesting that the standard deviation of the consumption component for the Keynesian case is about the same as for the estimated case. Although the residuals in the Keynesian consumption function are smaller than the residuals in the other case, the multiplier is quite a bit higher (0.85 as against 0.62). The big difference between the two cases is in the size of the other component. Again, because the multiplier is lower for the the estimated case and higher for the Keynesian case, the other component is larger for the Keynesian case. The Keynesian case reconciles a larger other component with a consumption component of about the same size by invoking a lower correlation of the two components. The negative correlation permits the sum to have the same standard deviation (the known standard deviation of the change in real GNP) even though one of the components is more variable.

8.10 Other Estimates

Estimates for other time periods and other specifications have convinced me that the basic findings of this paper are robust. First, estimates for the entire period, the interwar period, and the postwar period are

Entire period, 1920–82:

$$\Delta c_t = -0.16 \, \Delta y_t$$
$$(0.09)$$

SE: $47 billion; D-W: 1.37

$$\Delta x_t = -0.54 \, \Delta y_t.$$
$$(0.18)$$

SE: $96 billion; D-W: 1.78

For both equations, the considerable extra variance from the extraordinary level of military spending during World War II helps to reduce the sampling variation without changing the coefficients much.

Interwar period, 1920–42:

$$\Delta c_t = -0.13 \, \Delta y_t$$
$$(0.24)$$

SE: $70 billion; D-W: 1.31

$$\Delta x_t = -0.50 \, \Delta y_t$$
$$(0.50)$$

SE: $144 billion; D-W: 1.75

Postwar period, 1947–82:

$$\Delta c_t = -0.11 \, \Delta y_t$$
$$(0.20)$$

SE: $23 billion; D-W: 1.78

$$\Delta x_t = -0.36 \, \Delta y_t.$$
$$(0.41)$$

SE: $46 billion; D-W: 1.94

8.10.1 Results for a Direct Measure of Work Effort

In his comment on the version of this chapter presented at the conference, Angus Deaton suggested that the negative findings for the equilibrium model might be the result of the use of GNP as a measure of work effort. Because GNP might measure the result of other productive factors, including pure good luck, and these other factors reasonably might be positively correlated with consumption, the consumption/GNP relation might be more positively sloped than is the consumption–work effort relation.

To check this possibility, I repeated the analysis with full-time equivalent employment in place of real GNP. I detrended the series by its own exponential trend and rescaled it to equal real GNP in 1982. Application of two-stage least squares to the relation of the first difference of consumption to the first difference of employment, with the change in military spending as the instrument, for the periods 1930–42 and 1947–82, is

$$\Delta c_t = -0.10 \, \Delta y_t.$$
$$(0.18)$$

SE: $41 billion;   D-W: 0.91

Again, the structural slope is slightly negative but not nearly negative enough to fit the equilibrium hypothesis. The hypothetical value of -1 is strongly rejected.

8.11   Conclusions

A simple structural relation between GNP and consumption is a feature of two major theories of economic fluctuations, though the theories differ dramatically in most other respects.

In the Keynesian analysis, the consumption function slopes upward, so in principle the positive correlation of GNP and consumption could be explained purely by forces other than shifts in consumption behavior. Nonetheless, my results show that shifts in the consumption function are a source of overall fluctuations in a Keynesian analysis. In the first place, even the Keynesian consumption function has residuals, though they are smaller than the residuals from the equilibrium or estimated c-y relationships. In the second place, exactly because of the Keynesian multiplier process operating through a positively sloped consumption function, the consumption disturbances are much more strongly amplified than they are in the equilibrium or estimated models.

In the equilibrium theory, the relation is the expansion path of the work/consumption choice. The public is free to pick a point along the path in response to economic conditions. Shifts in government tax and spending policies and shifts in investment and net exports will move the economy along its negatively sloped c-y schedule. If ever GNP and consumption move together, it is the result of a shift in the consumption schedule. Because consumption and GNP frequently move together, random shifts of the consumption/work schedule must be a *dominant* part of the equilibrium explanation of cyclical fluctuations.

In the Keynesian model, an increase in military purchases should raise GNP and raise consumption. In the equilibrium model, an increase in military purchases should raise GNP and lower consumption. The data for the past six decades examined in this paper seem to split the difference—consumption is unaffected by military purchases, whereas GNP rises. Hence the estimate of the slope of the *c-y* relation inferred through the use of military purchases as an instrument is about zero. In the compromise economy (which does not have a theory to go with it), random shifts in consumption are an important source of overall fluctuations.

Notes

I am grateful to Olivier Blanchard and Ben Bernanke for comments and to Valerie Ramey for expert assistance.

References

Altonji, Joseph G. 1982. The intertemporal substitutian model of labour market fluctuations: An empirical analysis. *Review of Economic Studies* 49: 783–824.

Anderson, Barry L., and James L. Butkiewicz. 1980. Money, spending, and the Great Depression. *Southern Economic Journal* 47: 388–403.

Barro, Robert J. 1981. Output effects of government purchases, *Journal of Political Economy* 89: 1086–1121.

Barro, Robert, J., and H. I. Grossman. 1976. *Money, employment and inflation*. London: Cambridge University Press.

Barro, Robert, J., and Robert G. King. 1982. Time-separable preferences and intertemporal-substitution models of business cycles. Working Paper 888, National Bureau of Economic Research.

Flavin, Marjorie A. 1981. The adjustment of consumption to changing expectations about future income. *Journal of Political Economy* 89: 974–1009.

Friedman, Milton, and Gary S. Becker. 1957. A statistical illusion in judging Keynesian consumption functions. *Journal of Political Economy* 65: 64–75.

Garber, Peter M., and Robert G. King. 1983. Deep structural excavation? A critique of Euler equation methods. Technical Paper 31, National Bureau of Economic Research.

Hall, Robert E. 1978. Stochastic implications of the life cycle–permanent income hypothesis: Theory and evidence. *Journal of Political Economy* 86: 971–988.

Hall, Robert E. 1980. Employment fluctuations and wage rigidity. *Brookings Papers on Economic Activity* 1: 91–123.

Hall, Robert E. 1981. Intertemporal substitution in consumption. Working Paper 720. National Bureau of Economic Research.

Hall, Robert E., and Frederic S. Mishkin. 1982. The sensitivity of consumption to transitory income: Estimates from panel data on households. *Econometrica* 50: 461–481.

Kendrick, John. 1961. *Productivity trends in the United States.* New York: National Bureau of Economic Research.

Long, J. B., and C. I. Plosser. 1983. Real business cycles. *Journal of Political Economy* 91: 39–69.

MaCurdy, T. 1981. An empirical model of labor supply in a life cycle setting. *Journal of Political Economy* 89: 1059–1085.

Mankiw, N. Gregory, Julio J. Rotemberg, and Lawrence H. Summers. 1982. International substitution in macroeconomics. Working Paper 898, National Bureau of Economic Research.

Mayer, Thomas. 1980. Consumption in the Great Depression. *Journal of Political Economy* 86: 139–145.

Office of Management and Budget. 1983. *Federal government finances: 1984 budget data.* Washington, D.C.: Office of Management and Budget.

Temin, Peter. 1976. *Did monetary forces cause the Great Depression?* New York: Norton.

Index